ACE THE
TOEFL
ESSAY (TWE)

ACE THE
TOEFL
ESSAY (TWE)

Everything You Need for the Test of Written English

TIM AVANTS

SOURCEBOOKS, INC.®
NAPERVILLE, ILLINOIS

Copyright © 2007 by Timothy Avants
Cover and internal design © 2007 by Sourcebooks, Inc.
Sourcebooks and the colophon are registered trademarks of Sourcebooks, Inc.

This publication is designed to provide accurate and authoritative information in regard to the subject matter covered. It is sold with the understanding that the publisher is not engaged in rendering legal, accounting, or other professional service. If legal advice or other expert assistance is required, the services of a competent professional person should be sought.—*From a Declaration of Principles Jointly Adopted by a Committee of the American Bar Association and a Committee of Publishers and Associations*

All brand names and product names used in this book are trademarks, registered trademarks, or trade names of their respective holders. Sourcebooks, Inc., is not associated with any product or vendor in this book.

Published by Sourcebooks, Inc.
P.O. Box 4410, Naperville, Illinois 60567-4410
(630) 961-3900
Fax: (630) 961-2168
www.sourcebooks.com

Library of Congress Cataloging-in-Publication Data

Avant, Tim.
  Ace the TOEFL essay (TWE) / Tim Avants.
    p. cm.
  ISBN 978-1-4022-0843-0 (trade pbk.)
 1. Test of English as a Foreign Language. 2. English language—Textbooks for foreign speakers. 3. English language—Ability testing. I. Title.

PE1128.A93 2007
428.2'4—dc22

                                    2007024990

Printed and bound in the United States of America.
SB 10 9 8 7 6 5 4 3 2 1

Contents

Preface

Dear Reader,

This book is designed as a crash course for the TOEFL essay exam, sometimes called the TWE, Test of Written English.

***ACE the TOEFL Essay* has two fantastic components that are sure to help you get the score you want:**
  1. Outlines of exactly how to write essay exams, with transitional sentences, evidentiary statements, and every other type of expository element formatted in graphics.
  2. Ten real sample essay exams written by a university professor in response to ten real sample essay questions.

Furthermore, there are twenty pages dedicated to punctuation, including hundreds of examples. In addition to the ten real essay exams (model answers), a separate section explains six different patterns of development for essay writing; each pattern (except the first) with its own sample essay, highlighted for speedy reference, points out the cues to look for in essay questions and demonstrates how to respond in the essay answers. Plus, an irregular verb list and supplements on confusing adjectives, nouns, and adverbs provide the lost TOEFL student worlds of information at a glance.

In addition, <u>**a complete grammar section**</u> guides, pushes, and pulls the student to complete understanding. Sentence structure is dissected, pointing out every component and stressing the way words change functions as they change positions in sentences.

Furthermore, exercises drill the student on every facet of the test, with detailed explanations of the answers. This text includes everything, but the student can go straight to essays or points of grammar for easy reference.

Taking the Test of Written English

Included are ten model essays written by a real college professor in response to ten *real* sample essay questions, designed to get you the highest score possible on the TOEFL essay exam.

This book exists for one reason: to give you example after example of ideal TOEFL essays. The test calls for the knowledge of very distinct patterns of development—in other words, the way one must answer the essays. These patterns are often overlooked, and students find themselves simply writing for the allotted amount of time; this method is too unpredictable and unfortunately requires luck for any chance of success. Your success involves three steps. First, identify the pattern of development the essay question calls for. Next, write the essay in a very structured format (given here). Finally, have a backup plan if time runs out; your backup plan should include knowledge of how to mix and match your patterns of development. Look inside and learn.

PART I:

Writing the Essay

Patterns of Development

Simply put, a pattern of development is the method you employ to write a paper. These patterns are very simple to learn. Fortunately, they do not take much time, and employing them gives you the advantage needed to earn that outstanding score on the essay section of the TOEFL. Understand this: every essay question is worded in such a way that it requires a specific manner of response. The TOEFL reviewers do not care about the personal details in your response, but they do look for coherence in your answer. For example, one question from the TOEFL could ask, "Which would you prefer, a traditional home or a modern home?" Believe me, no one cares what your personal preference is, but the scorer cares if you know that this question requires your answer to be in a comparison-contrast pattern of development. There are two different approaches to that pattern, hereafter called a **pod (pattern of development)**. Now, let's look at the process of scoring.

Scoring

The essay is graded by two people. Scores range from 0, for not answering the question you are given, to 6, the highest possible, which translates to 800. If there is a great difference between the two scores given, a third grader will be called in. Roughly speaking, if you receive a 4, you are above average.

Length

The length is 300 to 500 words. That translates to two handwritten pages or one typed page. The time limit is thirty minutes. Your time and your length all funnel into a set number of paragraphs for each type of question you could encounter. Therefore, set up the essays exactly as I have presented them, at least regarding the number of paragraphs and the number of sentences in the introduction of each type of essay.

Presentation

The book contains: (1) a general introduction to the types of pods, including outlines for easy reference and fast viewing; (2) a component on punctuation; and (3) real answers to real sample essay questions. In the third section, you will be given the essay question first. Then, I will identify the type of question. Next, the possible pods you may use will be listed in order of importance. For instance, if you see words such as *definition* or *comparison-contrast*, you should first employ the definition pod. If for some reason you are blank about how to do that, you can use the comparison-contrast pod. In addition, if you get halfway through the essay and go blank, you could rely on your back-up pod, which is comparison-contrast here, for an additional paragraph. The key is to look at the right words in the question itself and proceed from there.

CHAPTER ONE:

Essay Formats

This chapter deals with rough patterns for essays. These patterns are variable and therefore rough; later on, I include essays that answer specific TOEFL questions. Look over the outlines carefully, and familiarize yourself with the various essay elements, such as transitional sentences and phrases, evidentiary statements (ESs; i.e., ones that provide evidence of the points you develop in your paper), examples, types of topic sentences for different pods, types of thesis statements, and finally sentence structure, which is determined by your pod. Do not be intimidated. You are capable of earning a 6. Good luck.

(For further explanations, see the list of terms at the end of the book.)

Comparison-Contrast

When writing a comparison-contrast paper, use words that suggest a relationship of similarity or dissimilarity, such as *opposite, alike, unlike, in common*, or any other words with the same meanings. Be aware of signals that will give you ideas on how to address the topic. The ease with which a professor, or anyone else for that matter, reads a pod is based on the reader's ability to move back and forth from point to point, comparing each in a relatively short time. Such a point-by-point structure facilitates the reading of the pod, but the writing of the pod is usually time-consuming for the student. However, on the exam, the points are there and relatively easy to write out. Therefore, I suggest the point-by-point pod for exams, especially if the exam is only four paragraphs in length. As a final note, remember that the number of paragraphs in a paper is directly related to the number of ESs in the introduction. The ES is the sentence that provides evidence to support your thesis statement (ThS). The following example, though, features two ESs despite having only one paragraph in the body. This is a rare exception, and is only common in a point-by-point pod wherein the two topics are dealt with in the body of the essay together. It is commonly called an ABAB pod, because every sentence jumps back to the subject. For example, one sentence is about A and the next is about B. This allows the reader to compare the two items fairly well without loss of time, which is important to a grader who does a lot of reading.

Let's look at a point-by-point pod that deals with a tangible subject. The transitions will be highlighted so that you can see exactly how to glue the ideas together. First, look at the diagram below. With a point-by-point pod, you can look at the possibilities in several ways. Primarily, with a really short paper, the ABABABAB style works, but it fails if you have a longer paper, say around four to five typed pages. Plus, we do not want to have a singsong rhythm that becomes monotonous. This style may still work, but we can apply it to one topic, perhaps encompassing four to five sentences. Actually, the length is up to you.

The first example of this type of paper is set up in the following format: AAABBB. The sentences should be equally grouped. For now, look over the next paper. Note the places where I have written notes to you. I have highlighted the transitions so that you can observe how we manipulate our sentence structure, reader attention, and the focus on the content. This paper is a response to the following essay exam question: Which would you prefer, an older home or a modern home?

Point by Point: Comparison-Contrast

For the individual who puts stock in the old and traditional, the strength of foundation, and the grandeur of space, the traditional house may be the choice of a lifetime. [ES1] The motifs of style that have long been played out in today's market of prefabricated homes are existent in those structures that were popular in the past. In addition, [ES2] foundations were stronger in older houses, and they still are, even given the course of time. For whatever reason, older homes also tend to be [ES3] larger. *These points certainly warrant more discussion.* (TR)

Reader: Now, you can write the body two separate ways with the point-by-point pod. First, you can write the sentences in a point-by-point format—one sentence about A and one about B—until you complete the category or group of sentences that pertain to evidentiary statement number one (ES1), the statement that supports the thesis statement. Therefore, the first motif of style could be written about in the following manner.

NOTE:

The symbol ¶ indicates the start of a new paragraph, which includes the indentation, or space, of five letters. The paragraph below starting with the word The *is indented five spaces. A space is the size of a letter.*

The style of older structures carries the charm of aristocracy or the peace of the rustic countryside as compared to the assembly-like packaging of modern homes.

A. **Basically,** the shopper can choose from a variety in the market of older structures.

A. **For instance,** if one wants to wrap himself in the old world of the nineteenth century, he can search in the "secondhand" market.

A. **Moreover,** the buyer can choose from different time periods, haggle on prices, or even negotiate in the arena of remodeling.

B. **On the other hand,** modern homes are thrown up in a hurry, many having the same features.

B. **Along those lines,** most homes in a particular subdivision cost about the same, so variety is limited.

B. **Consequently,** if the buyer wants to stand out in the crowd, the modern home disallows much personal freedom.

Reader: You should see how the underlined phrases tie the ideas together, provide contrast among the points, and ultimately guide the reader. However, we could have set up the body's format in one paragraph with the alternating ABAB method.

A

B

A

B

Caution: You should not number or letter the sentences as we did here. I did that only to give you visual cues so that you see how things are glued together. Also, do not skip lines unless you start a new paragraph. From the arrangement of the sentences, we could easily pull out eighteen sentences from those three points. Writing complete essays will become infinitely easier than before with these methods. Did you catch how our transitions were always placed at the beginning of each sentence? It is an excellent idea to vary the positioning thereof. Let's go back to the alternating ABAB method and move the transitions around in the sentences.

For the individual who puts stock in the **old and traditional,** the strength of **foundation,** and the grandeur of **space,** the traditional house may be the choice of a lifetime. [ES1] The motifs of **style** that have long been played out in today's market of prefabricated homes are existent in those structures of yesteryear. In addition, [ES2] **foundations** were stronger in older houses, and they still are, even given the course of time. For whatever reason, older homes also tend to be [ES3] **larger.** *These points certainly warrant discussion.* (TR)

The style of older structures carries the charm of aristocracy or the peace of the rustic countryside as compared to the assembly-like packaging of modern homes. **Basically,** the shopper can choose from a variety in the market of older structures. Modern homes, **on the other hand,** are thrown up in a hurry, many having the same features. **But,** if one wants to wrap himself in the old world of the nineteenth century, he can search in the "secondhand" market, *usually finding what he wants in traditional structures, although doing so may take longer.* A lover of traditional motifs can choose from different time periods, haggle on prices, or even negotiate in the arena of remodeling. **Along those lines,** most homes in a particular subdivision cost about the same, so variety is limited. **Consequently,** if the buyer wants to stand out in the crowd, the modern home disallows much personal freedom.

NOTE:

The preceding paragraph has been changed only slightly, and this was to accommodate logic. If the paper is short, like a short essay test, the AB-AB pod is better; however, if the structure requires time and effort at home, the AAABBB-AAABBB pod is better. This is the second way to write a point-by-point pod, which includes writing several sentences about one point. Notice how the transitions hold it together. I moved the transition **on the other hand** *to medial position, reworded a sentence, and added a qualifier in italics. You must employ a variety of sentence structuring techniques to keep your reader involved. Face it: most people do not want to hear what you have to say anyway, so be sly; manipulate the reader's attention, and accomplish your goals.*

Refutation-Proof

The next pod is the **refutation-proof paper.** This pod stands out for tearing down arguments that have already been made. Also, it's used as a debating technique, which attests to its potential effectiveness. The refutation-proof paper has a very tight structure, but it's also very flexible, which means examples, illustrations, and transitions can be integrated within the structure of the paragraph. To refute means to talk against, and a proof is evidence that asserts the truthfulness of a statement. So, the refutation-proof paper refutes someone else's claim and then proves, or provides evidence of, why your refutation against another's argument is correct. This is accomplished by addressing someone's claim with a series of statements, refuting this claim, and then explaining why the claim is incorrect, vicariously stating your stance on the matter in the process. This pod is used in political science, many of the social sciences that deal with theoretical arguments, literature—which may be useful to the students of this text—and almost any field that involves new developments. Let's apply this pod to a normal composition class, regardless of the level. It is quite common for the professor to assign specific readings, and, because many students frequently complain about their inability to come up with a topic to write about, a midterm or final examination may include an in-class assignment about the readings. For example, a professor could pick out the argument (main idea) of a piece and tell the students to comment on that argument, or there could be five questions to choose from, all including a common theme about the same topic, each question coming from the same or even different writers. The student should be prepared for any combination on an essay exam; therefore, the refutation-proof pod is quite handy to have in your arsenal.

In the following refutation-proof pod, the introduction summarizes the other writer's argument, the argument you will tear down in your paper. These statements are the ESs in the introduction. Just as in the other formats, the ESs come down, are reworded, and become the topic sentences of each paragraph. But, in direct contrast to the other formats, the sentences in the remainder of each paragraph tell why the topic sentence is wrong. Therefore, in essence, the paragraph acts as disclaimer to the topic sentence. There are two ways to approach this pod from here.

I. ¶ Topic Sentence = your idea how they err (Thesis statement)
   1. His idea
   2. His idea

Transitional Statement
¶ Topic Sentence (1 = TS [reworded])
  A. Your idea
  B. Your idea

C. Your idea

D. Your idea

Transitional Statement

¶ TS = 2 (His idea, reworded)

  A. Your idea

  B. Your idea

  C. Your idea

  D. Your idea

  TR Sent.

¶ Conclusion = Summing Up = Your Ideas

II. ¶ Topic Sentence = your idea, Qualify, Sweeping

  1. His idea + Qualifier

  2. His idea + Q + Adj.

  3. His idea + Q + Adj.

  4. His idea + Q + Adj.

  Transitional Statement

¶ Topic Sent. (1 = TS [reworded])

TS = S + V + Adj. + His idea

  A. Your idea

  B. Your idea

  C. Your idea

  D. Your idea

  Transitional Statement

¶ TS = 2 (His idea, reworded)

TS = S + V + Adj. + His idea

  A. Your idea

  B. Your idea

  C. Your idea

  D. Your idea

  TR

¶ TS = 3 (His idea, reworded)

TS = S + V + Adj. + His idea

  A. Your idea

  B. Your idea

       C. Your idea

       D. Your idea

       TR

  ¶ TS = 4 (His idea, reworded)

  TS = S + V + Adj. + His idea

       A. Your idea

       B. Your idea

       C. Your idea

       TR

  ¶ Conclusion = Summing Up = Your Ideas

It is best to cut the preceding down to fit the necessary length require-ment, perhaps even by 30% in the body.

Remember: We can always add to this, and we can always take away from it.

Cause-Effect

In academia, the cause-effect pod is probably the most common, along with the comparison-contrast. Look for words that suggest a connection between items, words that link, such as *cause, reason, effect, result,* and *lead to.* One can write short and long essay questions and term papers, as well as combine the cause-effect with other pod(s) for longer projects. When students complain to me that they cannot think of anything to write, I always tell them to think of something they hate right this minute. That is not so hard, because we all have something that really irritates us. If you can think of something you hate, it is probably existent as you read this. Think of how that thing developed into being. By tracing its development, you have come up with half of the battle in a cause-effect pod. We must be careful, however, that we do not have glitches or gaps in our logic. This is the most common problem I, as a professor, read in the papers of my students. To ensure that you don't make these same mistakes, see the chapter on logical fallacies. We also want to have a tight structure in regard to the time link between the causal factors and the effect in our paper. What do I mean by that? Do not try to explain the existence of racism, its origin, the development over time, and the status of it now in the United States in a paper of only two pages. A task like that calls for more space. Try to narrow the topic down. For example, you may want to trace the rise in racism within a particular cross section of the United States or the development of one motif of racism. When you narrow your topic, your paper will be more credible. Further, you can concentrate on a particular aspect you know more about to begin with. Mostly, though, you avoid broad generalizations for which graders usually take off points. Let's continue to think about and include our ESs in the introduction. These ESs will be the factors in a giant causal chain that runs through the paper, all leading to the effect that we, the writers, thoroughly hate or love—you decide. The effect should be in the thesis statement of your introduction. Basically, we will work backward, beginning with the effect and discussing the factors that lead to it. With this approach, the reader does not have to search for the thesis of your paper, nor does he need to wait until the end to discover what you truly think about the situation. Keep in mind that you never want to lose the reader. You want to guide him, but in order to do that you must keep him involved in the reading, especially if the reader is your grader.

¶ TS = Effect (Intro.)
2. ES
3. ES ∇
General to specific
TR = 1-2-3-4. This is the causal chain in order,
sufficing as the transitional sentence.

¶ TS = 2
Example
TR
¶ TS = 3
Example
TR
¶ TS = 4 (can put #4 with conclusion)
Value judgment
TR
¶ Δ Specific to general (Concl.)

We move back and forth from general statements to more specific statements at the beginning, because we are describing a general effect of that specific behavior. In the conclusion, we move from the specific to the general, because the body has detailed the specific behavior that becomes the causal factors.

The following introduction looks like this:

TS = Effect

1-2-3-4

1 = ES 1

2 = ES 2

TR

SAMPLE

Cause-Effect

Lifting weights can have a comprehensive effect on one's well-being. One may very well experience an immediate difference in **endurance,** leading to an increase in **appetite,** in turn fighting off sickness through good diet, and culminating in marked levels of **strength.** Often, beginners say they feel increased energy throughout the day. The relationships between food, feeling, and appearance are inseparable. In time, those same people love to look in the mirror, because the positive gains are surely notice-able. This is information that certainly needs to be shared.

Lifting weights has so many positive results, but one that is shocking to many people is how quickly a person improves his energy levels. _**For instance,**_ in as little as two weeks, the average Joe can significantly increase his endurance. That _**means**_ more energy at the end of the day. As a result, he could take extra class-es at night. A night workout schedule may _**also**_ take form. Instead of feeling wiped out after a day at work, one could engage in pro-ductive things such as community service or even volunteering to help a friend. _**More important,**_ by giving a little of oneself in the gym, a person can experience a return on his investment that can never be measured. *Exercise affects not only endurance level but also appetite.*

When an athlete, or almost anyone for that matter, fuels his body sufficiently and efficiently, his mind and body both reach new levels of competence. The small, pesky cold no longer nags as it did **_before_** those cleansing workouts, specifically **_because_** the body is cleansed of impurities through life-sustaining nourishment. Antioxidants whisk away the toxins in one's system. The blood circulation, **_as a result,_** experiences higher levels of oxygen; **_thus,_** one has more defensive ability. **_Hence,_** the body is hungrier **_than before,_** and any fuel, **_accordingly,_** might be used to maintain the system's requirements. **_There is a direct link between exercise, eating, and health._**

The single most significant milestone for many weight lifters is the ability to make progress in lifting. Most men say that to look in the mirror and see visible gains in muscle mass enhances their performance in the gym. Whether he is conscious of it or not, then, a guy feels better about himself when he can put more weight on the bar. It is no joke to surmise that all of the factors discussed herein are inextricably wound up together in one way or another. _The more a guy lifts, the stronger he gets. The stronger he gets, the more his body requires fuel. The more fuel he consumes, the more his muscle mass increases._ **_Then,_** he is drawn to the mirror, and he sees progress with time. _The more time he spends, the more gains he sees._ **_The cycle is certainly one big circle._**

To have a program is a good idea. To obtain whatever goals one has necessitates planning, commitment, and hard work. The main factor to persistence, many times, is one's ability to visualize what comes next, even though the net result may not be readily apparent. Diligence and visualization are the keys to implementing the cycle of success.

A Note on Transitions

In the first paragraph in the body, I varied the transitions as to initial and medial positions in the sentences. The transitional sentence at the end looks back at the preceding paragraph and looks ahead at the next topic.

Paragraph two does exactly the same thing, but the transitional sentence mentions the first two topics and links them to the third topic in the body. Finally, I changed the method in the body's last paragraph by focusing on cleft sentences to draw attention through the rhythm of the sentences. This suggests that all the elements influence each other. However, you can add to this with a longer assignment, sprinkling it with longer examples, real data, and even sources.

Comment: The cause-effect paper must have the links between points (causes and the effect) practically weaved together. If written well, and logically, the points will seem to naturally flow together. There will, though, always be a spot where something can be picked apart. But, we must remember that we are not writing a history or a pedagogical text in the course of one paper. Coherence, moreover, is an important key in anything one writes. If you are writing a scholarly piece, and you know that there are other existing bodies of criticism, ones that stand in contention to what you think, that which you have espoused, it is common to give a polite nod in your work; this suggests you are aware that many opposing points of view are out there. Give only a polite nod, however. The paper is yours, and do not feel obligated to delve into opposing arguments at any length unless your work is based on direct refutation of another's work.

What Types of Words to Employ

The **audience** plays a huge factor in determining the <u>development</u> of a paper. Development of a paper includes the **types of words** the writer employs; for instance, one may talk in <u>abstract terms</u>, or, if talking about the destruction of property, one could use <u>concrete language</u>, calling it *vandalism*—as opposed to a generalization like *maladjusted behavior*. **Word usage,** commonly termed **diction,** is linked directly to the **purpose** of the writer, which is certainly wrapped up with the reason why an audience exists in the first place. The same writer or speaker speaking to the same exact audience on a different day about a different topic may use completely different language than before, and this is due to the matter discussed at the meeting and the purpose of the writer/speaker. If the writer/speaker wants to excite the emotions of his crowd, he will probably speak in emotive appeals. Emotive appeals, abstract language, concrete language, and descriptions all set the **tone** of the writing or speech. Everything has a link, some sort of a glue that bonds them together. The purpose of the writer, whom he talks or writes to, why, how, where, and when all determine how things are bonded together. ***One could argue that this occurs in different ways:*** the audience determines the approach of the writer, and the purpose of the writer determines who his audience is, and, vicariously, the diction and the tone fall into place from there. The answer to that is subjective. If I am a college student, the audience, my professor, determines the purpose of my writing: passing the course. But, if I am a professional writer, I myself decide who my audience is by choosing where I sell my work. We need to prepare ourselves to write for different purposes, particularly seeing that a lifetime of writing is ahead.

Audience, succinctly defined, includes anyone who is paying attention. The person sitting at a stoplight, in the loosest of definitions, is the audience of that stoplight. We are the audience of billboards, commercials, radio announcements, the nurse, the doctor, and family members. When my attention is directed to a source for a brief instant, even unconsciously, I become an audience. Whether my attention remains fixed depends on my purpose. Whether the source, if it is a person, of course, continues to vie for my attention depends on his motivation. If he's a pushy salesman or a beggar, most likely he'll have a plan to keep me there and maybe draw me closer. This plan, devised at that exact minute or with a rehearsed format, is rooted in his goal. He has his goals, and I have mine. They have to meet in order for ultimate success to occur. Take, for example, the beggar. If a guy is in a hurry, and he's approached by the beggar, the scene may play out as follows.

The businessman, late, glanced repeatedly at his watch. He stood nervously at the corner, beaten by the whip of an arctic blast, waiting, waiting for that stupid, incompetent bus driver, twelve minutes behind. A haggard, broken, old homeless man about ten paces away limped over, eyes fixed on the businessman at the corner, who by now was shivering, staring at and tapping on his watch. The old man, the bushy, dirty, old beggar, tapped the waiting passenger on the shoulder. The businessman, caught unaware, turned suddenly, and the two stood face-to-face. The beggar, surprised that he'd startled the man, stood there and looked at the other, speechless. The businessman stepped back and surveyed his face, taking in the cracks, the sullen eyes, the bits of something that were caught in the old man's beard, and the snot around the nose. The old man lifted his hand, palms up, and started to say something, but he began to cough instead. Behind him, the businessman heard the roar of a big engine and the screech of brakes. He didn't turn but remained in that position, just staring. A flake of snow dropped on the businessman's face. It was cold. The door of the bus opened. The businessman turned and got on the step, but he stood there, looking back. The old man never moved. He whispered a half audible, "Please." The businessman stepped down, walked over to the man, grabbed his filthy hand, and then threw an arm around his shoulder. They looked at each other, and a world of apathy and a world of bitterness dissolved in a matter of seconds. The younger said to the older, "Let's go get something to eat."

Any method of saying something relates to diction. Authors are constantly scrutinized for their ability to say something and how they say it. One uses flowery language, the other directs the reader with a pedantic style, and another uses logic. Most people probably have an innate sense of verbalizing their feelings. Certain people click by saying very little at all. Ernest Hemingway has been heralded as the tough-guy writer who conveyed volumes in his writings through short, choppy sentences. The reader has to dig for the truth, a motif of twentieth-century modernist literature. This dig for the truth, as it is routinely called, involves looking for symbols, for double meanings in the diction, and at how the sentences are structured, among many other elements. Similarly, the tough guy on television rarely says much. Think of some actors. Chuck Norris, Jean Claude Van Damme, and Sylvester Stallone rarely get into long conversations. Of course, some tough-guy characters do, like Bruce Willis with his humor. Depending on the purpose and the particular approach one uses to convey his ideas, elaboration may or may not be appropriate. Hypothetically, if I write about gang violence in the local neighborhood, and I relate the story of the death of a five-year-old girl, I would definitely describe how her little, innocent body was brutally torn apart and how the gangsters laughed raucously as they sped away. Why? I want the public to know the putrid, hateful, callous behavior that takes place so frequently. These types of descriptions would involve very graphic detail with concrete language. On the other hand, descriptions of moral issues include abstract, intangible, untouchable things, because morality is abstract. Certainly, some topics allow the integration of the two. Most of the things we read have an integration of sorts. Again, everything depends on the purpose of the writer and for whom he is writing. The writing style, degree of elaboration, word choice, and syntax reflect on the tone.

The tone is the attitude the reader has toward the writer, perceived only by the author's written word. It may be wrong or misinterpreted, but it is valid. A child says something to be funny, but the parent takes it as insubordination. This is a perfect example of why choosing the correct words is so important. An author may write in short, choppy sentences throughout a piece and, at the end, discuss the immorality of something very minor in a long, complicated structure. One could interpret this style and the writer himself two ways. He is viewed as condescending or genuinely concerned. His point strikes home if he is read with understanding, but, if not, his attempt is futile. Consequently, one should keep the same style all the way through the text. If changing style is absolutely necessary, using appropriate diction will ensure that the change is evident to the audience. Sudden changes often disorient the audience. Although the structural patterns, topics, and transitional sentences are in order, it takes only one paragraph to tear down all the progress achieved.

Summing up, it is obvious that writers influence the audience and vice versa. Whatever the situation, the style of writing is set by the ideology and demographics of the audience. The aim of the writer dictates what tools he works with, such as diction, structure, pods, and the tone that shines through the finished product. All of these elements are inextricably connected. A relationship exists between every one of them. In the final analysis, the combinations are limitless, and only the writer knows exactly where he wants to go. **You have a very simple rule to follow: write about abstract things in very concrete examples.**

The extended definition paper uses abstract diction and concepts quite frequently.

Extended Definition

Look for words such as *call, appear to be, seem like, act like, define, say that,* and *may possibly be.* This pod prepares you for a lot of questions that deal with other people's opinions. It is called an extended definition because it adds to the generally accepted definition of a thing. Look for sentences that begin with "Some people say…." Look over the pod(s). The transitions are the same guiding light for your TOEFL grader.

¶ TS = General Definition + your idea (Compound Sent.)
1. ES
2. ES

TR
¶ TS = 1. Reworded
∇

Example
TR
¶ TS = 2. Reworded
∇

Example
TR

TR
¶ Δ
Concluding statement

Another Definition Paper

¶ TS = General Definition + your idea (Compound Sent.)
1. ES Note: 1–3 can be facets of your idea; thus
2. ES the paragraphs in the body don't require an
3. ES ex. in each. They can be replaced by comparisons
   TR and contrasts.

¶ TS = 1. Reworded
∇
comp-cont
TR
¶ TS = 2. Reworded
∇
comp-cont
TR
¶ TS = 3. Reworded
∇
Example
TR
¶ ΔΔ
Concluding statement

The next paper follows this pod. Everything is always interchangeable. These are guidelines to follow, like a workout routine. They are not written in stone. When we think in patterns, we can see writing and grammar as sets of patterns and not only as a group of words to grapple with.

Extended Definition

<u>Most people think compassion is feeling sorry for others when times are bad, but true compassion is feeling the pain of another individual. Empathy is the true earmark that separates the majority of those who see the pain of another and those who feel the pain of another.</u> Sharing the burden of a friend when life is so heavy demonstrates empathy. Consistency lingers on in those who feel that friend's pain. A closer look will reveal the differences in what most people think and a few actually know.

Placing oneself in another's spot is difficult, especially if one can only imagine how bereft the other feels. Suffering the death of a child is a prime example. When a person outlives his own child, an intolerable heaviness pervades every breath. It is easy to engage in idle conjecture, offer consolatory remarks, and even extend a hand in friendship. Often, we watch older people endure the loss of a spouse, and we feel sad, because they are acquaintances or family. After the funeral, we go our own way, with a pat remark, often sincerely given, and we go home, kick our feet up, and forget. Across town, Martha is wandering aimlessly, hearing Fred's voice, but he is not actually there. But Martha's friend, who buried her husband three months earlier, feels the pain all over again as she slips into bed. She can feel that same exact pain, because she suffered the same exact loss. She has been there. Martha's daughter does not feel like Martha does, because she lost a father, whereas Martha lost a lifelong partner. The pains are not equal. <u>The people who only see the pain and feel sorry for the bereaved whisper to themselves, deep in their hearts, that Martha should move on. But the one who suffered the same pain tries to be near the phone and help out in any way possible</u>.

To take the weight eases the load in a time of tragedy. Helping out hurting people is good, but they need more than that. To actually step under the burden means more than giving a hand. Only the bereaved can feel that complete loss at that exact time, but shouldering the responsibility means paying bills, buying groceries, setting appointments, and tending to things never thought of by those who watch from the outside. Sharing the burden is to actually live through part of the pain, even taking more than could ever be expected. It lightens the weight that virtually crushes the life out of someone with such a loss. Taking that responsibility transcends the menial tokens, the gestures, offered from duty, done in public, and displayed in formality. In contrast to duty, love is continuous, and the majority sleep when the knowledgeable attend to the burden of their friend.

Veterans of death, divorce, and other life-shattering events usually continue to help others, the victims, until they see the strength start to return. Most people never understand, at least until they go through it, the lingering effect of such catastrophes. But the ones who went through it do, and they are usually the ones to count on in the midst of sorrow. Day after day, these same faces drop by, bring things, go to the store, and go to the post office. They realize how physically debilitating sorrow is. For example, it is quite common to hear of a married person who dies, and, shortly thereafter, the spouse dies, also. Often, the surviving spouse does not have anyone to keep coming by, checking on things, and making sure the seemingly trivial things are not choking the survivor. The deluge of responsibilities can and does become overwhelming. Every small item to deal with hits like a sledgehammer or cuts like a razor, pushing one ever closer to the very last breath. That is why Martha's friend never accepts no for an answer. She never asks Martha if help is wanted. She simply helps.

Feeling sorry for someone is never equal to feeling the pain that someone feels. Taking up the slack is never on a par with taking over the reins and actually doing the work for someone who is having a hard time. Helping out is too brief. Helping up adds a reinforcement, a restrengthening of the old structure. But the work must be consistent for the structure to hold. Too much weight could cause the whole thing to tumble down.

End

NOTE:

The contrasts in the body's first two paragraphs are underlined, along with the example in the last paragraph of the body, just as it is set up in the diagram. If you feel lost, consult your patterns, and you have a ready-made formula.

Division-Classification

This pod is useful when working with divisions and subdivisions. It is used for reports, persuasive papers, lists, and a variety of other informative formats. If you have an essay exam and a lot of material to organize, employ this pod. Like the other formats, we can add to the following pod(s), and we can take away. How one sets up his particular format depends specifically on how much material he has to work with. First, you state a general division of items. From there, divide the items into smaller groups, classifying each group by characteristics that readily identify them. A simple introduction looks something like this: People (Gen. Div.) can be classified into several categories. Most are apathetic. Some try to help. But, by far, the smallest group is made up of those who will actually go out of their way to help a stranger. We could subdivide more if there were more groups or if the paper were extremely long. View the two following pods.

¶ TS = Names general division under which several groups are categorized.
1. Subcategory
2. Subcategory
3. Subcategory
TR
¶ TS = 1
Detail/Describe
TR

¶ TS = 2
Detail/Describe
TR

¶ TS = 3
Detail/Describe
TR

¶ △ Δ
Concluding statement

Another D-C paper:
¶ TS = Names general division under which several groups are categorized.
1. Subcategory
2. Subcategory
3. Subcategory

TR

¶ TS = 1

1a

1b

1c

1d

TR

¶ TS = 2

2a

2b

2c

2d

TR

¶ TS = 3

3a

3b

3c

3d

TR

¶ △△

Concluding statement

Now we have the format to use with many subtopics of each category. Plus, I could add to this by comparing and contrasting the categories themselves or by adding an example to each paragraph. Then, expanding each paragraph is never a problem. This is the key to expanding a paper. Similarly, condensing a paper adheres to the same philosophy. Many professors will use the same topic and the same material from their master's theses to write the dissertation in order to get the PhD. They rework the material, adding here and condensing there. The difference between the two is about 100–150 pages.

Division-Classification Paper

¶ Thesis Statement: Two types of writing: (I) Exposition, (II) Persuasion.
   Ia. Periodicals Ib. Pedagogical Material
   IIa. Rhetoric IIb. Miscellaneous
   TR
   ¶ Ia & b
   TR
   ¶ IIa & b
   TR
   ¶ Conclusion

This is the highly condensed diagram of the next pod. It's possible to break up a and b of both categories and give them separate paragraphs, but the paper is so short that separate paragraphs are unwarranted.

D-C Sample Paper

SAMPLE

All writing falls into two categories: exposition and persuasion. Exposition includes periodicals and didactic material whose only purpose is to inform. Just across a blurred line of distinction sits persuasion, whose main purpose is to influence the reader to think a certain way or to do something, and this category includes rhetorical pieces along with a miscellany of others. Sometimes close scrutiny is required to distinguish exactly where a piece fits.

Periodicals include daily newspapers, monthly magazines, and quarterlies. Generalizing, we will assume that the primary objective of those that report the news is to inform, and these are the ones we are interested in. Any reputable news reporting agency, following the formal and ethical rules of reporting, tends to be objective and does not moralize or change the facts. The one end in mind is to report, giving the facts, with no personal stake involved other than to convey the information in an unbiased fashion. Of course, there are some that deviate from this norm, such as tabloid periodicals, but those are not in the present class. Texts are good examples of didactic material, that which is used to teach. The author tells the reader something, from a factual perspective, with no personal involvement in the outcome of the information. To qualify that statement, I must add that the author knows the truth, and the reader's acceptance of the information is good. If not, that is fine, too, because the information is generally accepted anyway. The author of a textbook is not trying to convince the reader that the author himself is right. He simply presents the information, and his responsibility is over, assuming that his other responsibilities as an educator are fulfilled prior to that. News stories, news broadcasts, weather forecasts, textbooks, encyclopedias, and reports all belong to this category. At times, differentiating between the categories of exposition and persuasion is extremely difficult. The method to categorize material is to question why the information is given. If the presenter benefits according to the belief the reader has in the content of the material, then the material is probably persuasive, or what is adjectivally referred to as argumentative. Students write arguments through term papers and essays. The most revered argument written in the age of reason comes in the form of rhetoric. Rhetorical writing and speech became an art, and it still is, actually. The aim is to persuade the thoughts and influence the actions of the reader and the listener. It involves cadence, assonance, consonance, and figurative language. Traces of these techniques are also seen in places such as theses, newspaper editorials, and advertisements. The most skillful professional, however, wants to influence the reader to believe, but without the reader realizing this belief has crept into being. For instance, proposals for big business involve research, perhaps costing millions of dollars. Then, a bid is made to obtain work or something equally beneficial, all with the express goal of achieving an end. Buying a car, for example, is a typical scenario where one may be convinced to buy through imagery and logic. Again, depending on the awareness of the reader or the listener, the consumer is pulled by, pushed from, and, at the very least, exposed to the art of persuasion. Looking at the barrage of what we are exposed to daily hones the skills of judging what we see.

Understanding the fine line that separates exposition and persuasion benefits people every day. The basic understanding emanates from a center of calm when we are hit by the desire to accept information thrown our way. Usually, the one throwing the information reveals why. Like getting to know someone, eventually it's not hard to observe and make value judgments, ones based in experience and in an informed decision-making process.

Example/Illustration

This pod is extremely simple, almost self-explanatory. Therefore, I will not include a sample paper, just a couple of different pods. One tries to prove a point through example, so presenting your argument and depending on only one example for proof will lead to fallacious logic. I suggest you include no less than three illustrations as evidence, more if possible. If, however, you want to relate a story or tell about something, but not necessarily prove a point, one example is fine. Otherwise, think of using examples as racking up evidence.

¶ TS
1. ES
2. ES
TR

¶ TS = 1 reworded
TR 9
Example
TR

¶ TS = 2 reworded
Example
TR

¶ TS = 3 reworded
Example
TR

¶ Conclusion: Rehash briefly the three lessons learned in the three examples.

 *NOTE:* *The transitions (TR), and forward to the next example in order to unify the illustrations, thereby making your argument coherent. Make sure the examples are definitely related. Plus, they may be incidents in different environments to prove how your point applies to more than one type of situation.*

The last illustrative pod is best when there is very little time to organize a plan of attack, such as on a test. Most test questions will require examples on an essay.

Example/Illustration Pod

¶ Thesis Statement
ES
ES
ES
TR
¶ TS=

Ex: = 1
Ex: = 2
Ex: = 3
Ex: =
Try to include examples which cover all three ESs
Ex: =
¶ Concl: 3–8 lines to sum up

 **NOTE:** *Transitional phrases are the links between the examples (e.g.,* first, then, next, to add to the above, finally*).*

Generally, this addresses a test question for disciplines such as history, sociology, and the humanities. They answer broad questions with broad answers yet include specific examples.

Ex: "Playing a game is fun only when you win." Discuss.

Your answers will naturally cover broad areas, but, through illustrations, it's possible to address several areas exactly and then throw up an umbrella to include the rest.

Process Analysis

The process analysis paper describes in detail how something is done. For example, some students write papers on how to write papers. Two major pods could be followed, but the length of the paper usually determines which one should be employed. We will not look at a sample paper, although the two patterns are included here.

The first pod is best if the paper is about 500 words. Use this, because it displays a tight structure, and that is usually what a reader looks for in these questions. Further, if the reader wants to access any particular step in the process without hassle, he can go directly to the introduction for guidance. The key to remember is to be concise. However, this is used if you have many small steps in the procedure.

¶ Thesis Statement

1. ES
2. ES
3. ES

TR indicating all steps are combined; therefore, only one paragraph may or may not be inclusive of all the steps (your decision).

¶ TS = ES1

A

B
C All substeps for #1
TR
¶ TS = ES2
A
B
C All substeps of #2
TR
¶ TS = ES3
A
B
C All substeps of #3
TR
¶ Conclusion: 3 sentences

NOTE: *This assumes that you have enough information to fill up this much space through this many substeps. If not, the next pod is better.*

In lieu of evidentiary statements, simply mention several major categories you want to touch on; for instance, in a paper on how to write a paper, mention that a connection exists between the audience and your approach. No less than three sentences here.

TR
¶ Broad Topic Sentence

Go through your procedure methodically, using words such as *next, after that, short-term result, long-term effect, additionally,* and so on. If you get lost or run out of ammunition, add a concessional statement or even several that say there are other ways. You can include one or two other approaches as padding for your paper, but keep on track, and write in simple sentences. You must have a line of coherence, one that sets forth clear steps on how to perform a procedure.

> TR
> ¶ Conclusion
> About three sentences

You may qualify that you included alternative ways to approach your procedure.

Transitions

Transitions effectively control the reader by controlling the flow of an argument. Transitions regulate the time during which a reader has an idea. After completing a paragraph, look at the structure. You should be able to see how much space you have given a particular subject. You should also easily recognize where you have made mistakes in logic or coherence. Specifically, if you have wavered on a particular subject, perhaps only talked around a subject, this is obvious to see by looking at the transitional phrases. Even speed-reading specialists teach that one must learn to focus on transitions, because they reflect a change in the structure of ideas. Again, to use the analogy of a road map, transitions signal the reader where he should go, and, if used effectively, control the reader's attention as well. Transitions can be single words, several-word phrases, clauses, sentences, or paragraphs. I have taught around the world, and the most common advice I give to students taking the TOEFL exam is to circle the transitional phrases on the Reading Comprehension part of the test so that they can easily follow the flow of the paragraph. Then, the transitions are especially easy to find when answering the questions about the reading. The same idea applies to writing. Learn the transitions, and your writing will empower you to write your way to academic success. Memorize the lists below.

Agreement: also, plus, in addition, further, furthermore, moreover, additionally, to add to that, next, in accordance with, accordingly, in agreement, finally, for instance, for example, in exemplification, exemplifying that, in point of fact, in fact, factually speaking, in terms of, and so forth, looking at the nexus between, in coordination with, along those lines, collectively speaking, generally speaking

Contrast: however, contrastingly, in contrast, on the other hand, to put it into perspective, from a different angle, nonetheless, nevertheless, but, yet, a catch to this is, sadly enough, as a hindrance, looking at the holdups, oddly enough, instead, in direct opposition

Result: as a result, as a consequence, consequently, thus, therefore, hence, thereby, resulting in, ultimately, in the end, finally, in the overall analysis, in hindsight, in retrospect, retrospectively, vicariously, the long-term effect, in hindsight, as a short-term result, significantly, as a major effect, effectively, heretofore, hereafter, thereafter

NOTE: *Some of these straddle different categories. In one particular example, they may signify a different meaning compared to another example in a different context.*

Tip: If you always think of yourself as actually being in the paper, you know instinctively where to point your reader. For example, if I talk about the effect of something up until the present time, I may use the word *heretofore.* From that point on, I could use the word *hereafter.* I am still talking about result, but I am pointing either backward or forward. Your papers always deal with the relationship of a certain time to another. This is imperative to remember for logical consistency. If you think of yourself like this in your own paper, your reader will probably not get lost, because he will have the road signs that tell him how he got there, where he is, and where he will go in the paper from there. Those road signs are the words, the transitions, which link. In addition, when a professor has any doubt about the content of your paper, he can go back and reread by simply following the transitions.

For now, let's think of our transitions as attachments at the front, middle, or end of our sentences. Our sentences are, in essence, radar controlled, guided by the transition. Start with thinking of the transitions at the beginning of the sentence; then, add from there. If the sentence doesn't follow the radar device, the sentence will be illogical, filled with static, and so will the logic of all of the sentences around it. They will collide, because our guiding force was not in sync with the rest of the unit. The following chapter deals with different pods most common in academia. We'll move through each paper carefully, methodically, looking at the structure, keeping an eye on how things cohere, where they fit together, and why. Remember: We add to and take away from these structures. There are endless combinations possible using these pods. For purposes of definition, *pod* refers to the particular name we give to the type of paper we write: for example, comparison-contrast, description, cause-effect, and many more are types of papers, named thus because of the pod employed. One of the main items we will keep looking at again and again is the transition. So, instead of devoting a chapter to it, we will refer to the transition when we change pods.

Now we have established a very basic foundation for the following pods. After the chapter on punctuation, you have a whole list of essays that are direct answers to sample TOEFL questions. Remember that you have numerous combinations to use when writing these essays, including a mix-and-match approach, which is mainly effective if you have a problem reaching the required length.

CHAPTER TWO:

Punctuation

The Comma

The comma is used to set off words, several-word phrases, or clauses.

There are two basic rules I like to use when determining when to put a comma in a sentence.

The Formal Rule

If you have an independent clause (IC), and something comes to the left of the subject, and it's not an article, and it's not an adjective, set it off with a comma.

> **Example: On the way,[we stopped at the store.]**
> **S–V**
> **IC**
> **The big boy ate the candy.**
> **Art.–adj.–S–V–art.–Direct Object (DO)**

There is no comma in the second example, because it does not follow the rule (the words before the subject are an article and an adjective). We said that the clause must be an IC. That means it must be able to stand alone. If not, it's not an IC. If it's not independent, it's either a sentence fragment or a dependent clause (DC). A DC will usually begin with a word that will make it depend on a subsequent sentence to complete the thought. For example:

When I was a boy, I ate candy.

DC–IC

The DC usually has a subject and a verb, and it is referred to as a subordinate clause. The subordinator makes an IC dependent. Generally, a subordinator is usually a preposition: *in, on, after, under, whenever, before, while, among, next, toward.*

Not all DCs necessarily have a subject and a verb, but, for the sake of discussion, we will talk in generalizations. Therefore, although a clause or phrase that comes before an IC may not have both a subject and a verb, we usually set it off by using both rules described here.

Along the banks, fires were glowing.

Around the bend, a truck had crashed.

In December, we stay in the house.

After dinner, we ate dessert.

Up the coast, there were many seagulls.

Under the table, the boy played carelessly.

The Gut Rule

Simply put, if there is no trauma, don't add a comma.

I don't want to oversimplify, but we can usually look at the sentence and determine what is pertinent information and what is superfluous. By doing this, combined with the formal rule, we can figure out where to put the comma.

For example: Today, I went to the store. Yesterday, I went shopping.

The important information comes after the comma in both sentences. It is not really important that the person went to the store today. Simply the fact that he went to the store is important. The same logic is true with the second sentence. Now, if I want to make the information of today just as important as the fact that I went to the store, I will integrate that into the structure of the IC. For example: I went to the store today. I went shopping yesterday. I want to eat chicken tonight.

Let's view these sentences in regard to how they are actually spoken. If the time tag is at the beginning of the sentence, there will be a slight pause in the sentence before I start to say the information in the IC. This pause is a change in tone that leads me to believe that I must include a comma. Note that the tone goes down where the comma is inserted, and it rises again after the comma in the IC.

Tone: _____~⌐⌐⌐ _____

Today, I went shopping.

I went shopping today.

Tone: _____

Tone and stress are two different things. I can stress a certain word, but that does not necessarily mean that I automatically put in a comma. Likewise, I now feel compelled to dispel a myth. Most of us were taught—and wrongly, I might add—to put a comma in a sentence if there is a pause. Well, that's not always true. Following that logic, let's look at an example. Let's assume that my wife saw me at the store with a beautiful woman, and she asked me about it after I made it home. Following the logic of the rule we are usually taught in elementary school, we would punctuate my reply with the commas indicated. Keep in mind that I will choose my answer very carefully to her question, because I will definitely live with my answer for the rest of my life.

Question: Who was that woman you were with at the store?
Answer: S,s,s,s,s,hh,he,ee ii,i,is,s,s,ss mm,mm,yy ff,f,ffr,rr,iiennd.
(She is my friend.)

I hope you get my point. So, let's forget about the rule that we must always put in a comma if there is a pause in a sentence. If there is no trauma, don't add a comma. We almost always need commas after transitional phrases, which we've discussed before, because they come before an IC.

Afterthought

An afterthought needs to come after an IC. It signals extra information, but at the end of a sentence. There may be contention with a professor about the use of commas in this regard, because only you can determine whether the afterthought is actually extra information or whether it is, in fact, pertinent.

We sat down and ate candy, *and old bread.*

I saw the man with one arm, *and also his dog.*

I ate the whole chicken, *then had dessert.*

We played football, *and basketball.*

However, a sentence with one subject and two predicates (verbs) or two objects does not need a comma. Ex: He ran and walked. He ate bread and cheese.

Appositive

An appositive commonly renames a noun, and it is usually set off by commas. The noun and the other phrase renaming or describing it have reference in common, one normally renaming another. Some appositives are not set off, and these are deemed restricted, because their address is directed (restricted) to only the noun or its equivalent next to it. Again, *restricted* means that one does not add any commas, because the description is restricted or limited to the word or phrase directly next to it.

Those set off with commas are nonrestricted.

The fat boy, <u>the one with the glasses</u>, sat on my ice cream.

I like sports, <u>namely boxing</u>, more than studying.

Her most outstanding characteristic, <u>being nice</u>, brought her luck.

One thing, <u>running</u>, is better than most anything I know.

He bought her a gift for her birthday, <u>a cruise</u>.

The man <u>Jon</u> lit a smoke.

The general, <u>Rommel</u> won the battle.

The underlined words are the appositives. All the underlined phrases rename or describe the noun before it, except in the fifth sentence, where *cruise* renames *gift*. Here, *a cruise* is an afterthought, so we offset it with a comma.

Interjections

We said before that interjections interrupt. I also said that they are utterly useless, and that is generally true, at least in the context in which we saw them. An interjectory phrase can be highly useful information, but it is, nevertheless, extra. It can be a transition that directs an argument, or it may comment somehow. For example:

1. I think, however, life is good.

2. She said, convincingly enough, that she was innocent.

3. I, oddly enough, feel tired.

4. He looked like, but I'm not sure, the man who shot the dog.

Explanations:
1. Here, ***however*** signals a change in the direction of a conversation.
2. ***Convincingly enough*** comments on the subject matter of the sentence.
3. ***Oddly enough*** comments on the content of the message.
4. The clause ***but I'm not sure*** interrupts to give extra information and comment on the content of the sentence.

 *NOTE:* *Because we have broken the structure of the sentence (i.e., interrupted it), we must set apart the interjections (phrases and clauses) with commas.*

Independent Clauses

When we join two ICs with a comma, we must connect them with a coordinating conjunction (c/c). These words act as c/cs when they connect two ICs; when moved in the superstructure (i.e., both clauses linked together to make one complete sentence), they may take on different functions. Hence, the c/cs are situated between the two ICs.

BOYFANS: but, because, or, yet, for, and, nor, neither, so

I went, but I didn't enjoy myself.

I want money, because I'm hungry.

I will go to Egypt, or I'll return home.

I ate, yet I'm still hungry.

For: Do not use this; it is somewhat archaic. He stayed behind, for he was ill. *For* generally has the sense of a causal relationship, but the indication of the relationship between the event in the first clause and that in the second is more ambiguous than with the usage of *because*. Plus, it is chiefly British English.

I walked a mile, and I lifted weights.

I won't run, nor will I walk. I don't drink alcohol, and neither does he.
(Notice the inverted word order in the second clauses with *nor* and *neither*.)

I drank coffee, and so did he. I wanted ice, so I went to the store.

Series of Things

When listing a series of things, commas are used between sentence fragments, single-word phrases, and descriptive phrases.

Sentence fragments:

I went home, ate some food, walked the dog, and went to bed.

I stayed up late, got up early, and worked out.

My son kicked the ball, cleaned the garage, and set up the basketball hoop.

I called the verb phrases sentence fragments, because they all lack a subject. Therefore, they can be linked by use of a comma. But, if they had subjects, we would need to add a c/c. They can be linked a different way, which we will discuss later. Always look for the subject and verb when punctuating a sentence, and you can determine how to set it up.

Single-Word Phrases

He sings, dances, and plays.

He bought an apple, a toy, paper, and a pen.

I saw Bob, Mary, and Ted.

 *NOTE:*

If there are three or more items, we need to put an article before the last item in the series. If there are only two items, we do not need a comma at all.

Descriptive Phrases

The big, fat, ugly bear ate the meat.

The old, rusty, worn-out plane crashed.

The oldest, prettiest, and most majestic tree was cut down.

 *NOTE:*

We put the commas between the adjectival phrases because they all modify the same noun, so if the adjectival is not describing the word in front of it, we must insert commas between them, unless, as in the last sentence, an adverb describes an adjective. Likewise, with the sentence fragments or the verb phrases, one subject is involved in several actions; thus, each particular unit must be set off by a comma.

Semicolons

Semicolons link ICs. Plus, they link sentence fragments in block language. Block language is used more with technical writing, but the occasion may be there within certain term papers.

Independent Clauses

To link two ICs with a semicolon suggests some sort of a causal relationship. The first clause acts as a cause, whereas the second clause is the effect.

I ate; I got sick.

She has her life; I have mine.

They went their way; we went ours.

The old man died first; his wife died within a month.

The superstructure itself could be diagrammed like this:
General Statement: Specific Statement
If we wanted to change the pattern of the sentences, we could rewrite them thus:

Because I ate, I got sick.

Since she has her life, I have mine.

Because they went their way, we went ours.

Because the old man died, his wife died.

This does not mean that all sentences fit into this category, but it's a good strategy to use when working with the semicolon in superstructures that contain only two clauses. This involves writing style and the ability to change your sentence structure.

Semicolon with a Series of Independent Clauses

Again, this is more common in technical structures, but academic writing requires the use of it, especially in term papers. In term papers, it's often necessary to work with series in quotes, especially if you include the support of many scholars or, perhaps even more common, if you refute specific contentions a scholar has concerning your topic. The series may be introduced with a colon.

Professor X contends Lord Tennyson's writing had a threefold function: primarily, it acted as a cathartic function after the sudden demise of his best friend; secondly, the repetition of his work vicariously honed his skills throughout the next thirty years, in spite of the silence; lastly, his writings acted as, and continue to do so, a bridge for contemporary scholars to glimpse into the mind of one of the most prolific writers the West has ever known.

Using the semicolon in this arrangement allows the writer to organize his work and that of others in a concise pattern. Conciseness is a valuable asset in an effective term paper. We want to use semicolons to link two ICs to set a very serious tone. To include a c/c sets a lighter and airier tone. Sometimes that's not appropriate to convey your message.

Reminder: The audience determines the diction used; the diction sets the tone.

Colon

Use the colon to (1) introduce a list or series of items and (2) to express extremely important information. The colon must follow an IC.

> I did three things: ate, exercised, and studied.
>
> I have had problems with the following functions: working with graphs, setting the tabs, and copying the text.
>
> He wrestled with three scenarios: it was necessary to find the brain tumor in time; the donor was dying; the consent form was lost.
>
> He wrestled with three scenarios: it was necessary to find the brain tumor in time, but the donor was dying, and the consent form was lost.

Tip: Capitalize the beginning of the information after the colon only if it includes an IC or if it is only one word. Also, each IC is capitalized in the series with the semicolon, because the semicolon acts like a period, signifying a terminal break in the continuity of that IC, whereas if we join the IC(s) with a c/c, the new IC is *not* capitalized In the last example, this sentence carries a less serious tone and less gravity than that of the preceding superstructure wherein the ICs are joined by semicolons. Furthermore, in formal writing, one needs to vary the sentence patterns; therefore, the use of semicolons should be used more frequently when dealing with structures like these. In the next structure, we need to follow our technical rule and our gut rule closely to determine where to put the commas. Think in terms of formality.

S–V–c/c–S–V / Sub. S–V

After the game, we went to the store, but we came home / *when it began to rain.*

Explanation: If you have an IC, and something is to the left of the subject, and it's not an article, and it's not an adjective, set it off with a comma. Here, the word *game* fits that description. So, we put a comma after the word *game*, because *game* is a noun. We put a comma before *but*, because *but* is a c/c that links two ICs. Looking at the DC, *when* fits the description at the beginning of our explanation. **However, *when* is a subordinator, so it's not set off by a comma.** A time word, usually one that indicates a duration of time, or a preposition before the subject tells us that we're dealing with a DC, which must be set off from the IC if it precedes the IC in the superstructure. Let's invert the structure of the previous sentence to exemplify the point.

IC

When it began to rain, we came home.

DC

Because the DC comes before the IC, it is set apart by a comma, which logically follows the gut rule: if there is no trauma, don't add a comma. The change in tone comes after the word *rain*, indicating that the most important information comes thereafter. But there is no change in tone between the word *when* and the word *it*. Generally speaking, if the DC comes before the subject of the IC, set it off; however, if the DC is integrated into the structure of the IC, as in the previous example, leave it alone, unless it is an afterthought. Here, there is a trauma after *rain*, so we do add a comma. Trauma is the gross disruption of continuity in stress.

When using the colon to express extremely important information, I equate using the colon with using the palms of your hands to slap someone in the chest. It's like saying, "Hey! Listen up!" I always give the analogy of two small children playing at school. However, one is a bully, and he begins to pick on the other one, thinking the smaller one will not fight back. The smaller one, knowing he must completely surprise the bigger one, pushes him with both hands as hard as he possibly can, thereby getting the complete attention of the bully. The principle is the same.

> I only want one thing: money!
>
> She is only one thing: a user.
>
> He only wanted to go one place: home.

It is permitted to capitalize *money* in the first example, but it is uncommon to use this construction. However, don't capitalize the other similar constructions, unless they carry enough weight to have an exclamation point at the end of the sentence. The colon stands in direct opposition to the dash in the comparison of importance.

Dash

Use the dash to set off something in the sentence that is unimportant. The item set off, then, is only extra information, and, accordingly, if it were left out of any of these sentences in a composition, the reader would not lose anything important.

> Walking to the store—any day—is relaxing.
>
> I bought a scarf—a green one.
>
> A little boy—one with glasses—fell off his bike.

We could say that a dash is better suited for use with unimportant interjections than is any other kind of punctuation.

Apostrophes

Apostrophes are used to show possession.

The boy's cat fell off the house.

The girl's coat was left at school.

The team's victory took them to the championship.

All of these are singular, so we have noun + apostrophe + *s*.
If we want to show possession of the plural form of a regular noun, we place the apostrophe after the *s*.
Noun + *s* + apostrophe.

The boys' dog died. (The dog belonged to more than one boy.)

The teams' losses sent them all home. (More than one team lost.)

The computers' abilities nowadays are astounding. (The many abilities of many kinds of different computers astound me.)

Possessive of Irregular Nouns

The children's toys were lost. (The toys that belonged to two or more children were lost.)

Children is the plural of *child*; therefore, the pattern used to make the possessive of a singular noun is followed.

I saw Jesus's picture. (There is only one Jesus here, so we follow the rule for a singular noun.)

I saw the Avants' house. (Avants is a family name, plural in this sentence. This means the house that belongs to all of the people in the Avants family. However, if I am talking about only one person named Avants, and only one person lives at that house, I use the pattern for a singular noun, regardless of the s on the end of the noun.)

That is Avants's house. (It belongs to Luke Avants.)

Apostrophe with a Plural Phrase

There are basically two ways to make this kind of phrase possessive. They are both correct.

That is John's and Tom's cat. (It belongs to both of them.)

That is John and Tom's cat. (It belongs to both of them.)

Sentence Fragments

The most common mistake with fragments is simply not attaching an afterthought to an IC.

I went to the store. _After the game_. Wrong!

Or

After the game. I went to the store. Wrong!

As we mentioned earlier, a clause must be able to stand alone in good form and be a grammatically complete structure to be an IC. A sentence fragment like this is like a grown kid. He is big enough to do what he wants, but he always comes home and asks for money; therefore, he is not actually independent at all. That is the way these fragments appear to you when you read your own material, especially immediately after you complete the assignment. So, when you proofread your papers, see if the construction in question can stand alone, without the assistance of any other sentences around it. If so, you have an IC. If not, you have some rewriting to do. If I came up to you and said, "After the game," and then walked away, you would think I was crazy. Also, when you proofread, read your sentence and examine the structure, not the ideas. You are too biased to try to read the ideas impartially. If you have any doubts, look to this chapter on punctuation for help. This is also true with papers. You should be able to cut out any given paragraph of a paper, and the paper should still make sense. Therefore, if you begin a paragraph with *this* or *that* in reference to something stated in the previous chapter, you have a big problem.

CHAPTER THREE

Sample Essays

Essay #1

Question: Movies and books can reflect the ideas and the spirit of a particular period. What have you learned about a place or its people from watching films or reading books? Use specific examples and details to support your response.

Answer pod: 1. Cause-effect 2. Example

Watching a movie may tell the viewer about the country in which it was made in a couple of ways. Primarily, he can see life in its natural environment. In addition, the viewer may understand the ideas the natives have about themselves. When he sees a movie, he gets complete information in unrehearsed form, leading to the ability to see how the people think about one another, and ultimately the viewer could integrate his ideas with those of the others.

The movie tends to relate information that is usually most effective to the viewer if it comes naturally. For example, the speech accent from a particular area of the country may automatically blend in with the script. If a movie is filmed in the northern part of a country where a particular accent is dominant, that accent may shine through with the extras in the cast. Also, depending on the type of movie it is, environment sometimes plays a giant role in depicting the daily life of that area. The Great Plains region of the United States, for instance, relies heavily on the dairy industry for its capital. This may be obvious in movies set in that geographical location. Further, it is evident in movies set in the South that certain crops generate jobs, skilled or unskilled; create production for textile plants; contribute to the trucking industry; and sustain the economy in many other aspects, as well. This leads to the information the moviegoer gets about the people.

Many movies stimulate conversation about a topic, perhaps an event from the past, that opens up feelings that are usually avoided in textbooks. The southern United States again provides adequate examples. In order to convey heartfelt resentment that one group harbored toward another, writers will include disparaging remarks, disturbing scenes, and even value judgments in the plots of movies. If the audience members watch closely enough, they can catch a wealth of information simply through the conversations. Plus, the movie producers and directors want to produce a lifelike situation, either to make a lot of money or to make a social comment. Consequently, the elements therein allow people to learn, much more so than by merely reading a book. These warrant some final consideration.

Close observation opens up new worlds in many ways. It can tell us things we would otherwise never know. Most often, we see more when we look and listen. Fortunately, movies give us that option, but it requires diligence.

Note to Reader: Count your sentences. Look at the length and the pattern. Compare this essay to the outline in the sections on pods. There is a causal chain, but we wrote in depth about only two of the four points; moreover, the causal chain acted as your transitional statement between the introduction and the first paragraph in the body. Therefore, we still have only four sentences in the introduction.

SAMPLE 2

Essay #2

Question: Compare and contrast learning by doing to learning by reading. In your opinion, which is better? Explain.

Answer pod: 1. Comparison-contrast (point by point) 2. Definition 3. Cause-effect

Generally speaking, learning by doing affects one more on a personal basis compared to learning from books, which provides a more practical use in a high-tech world. The personal knowledge may come from pain, or it may even define an individual. On the other hand, book learning gives benefits regarding career development and more informative material. These benefits need examination.

Regardless of the source of knowledge, it is always wise to make it serve the learner. Experience gives an edge many times in areas of dealing with people and problems, things people do not particularly look forward to. However, though information from books includes how to deal effectively with people and certain kinds of problems, that information does not measure up to experience. Experience teaches how to be patient in certain circumstances. Although a book might actually suggest that patience is beneficial, it can never describe or teach the way experience can. In addition, having been through crises, any individual should be better equipped to handle the next crisis that may happen along. Plugging that same scenario into the book, a text can never prepare the reader for the loss of a child; there is no comparison between reading about it and living it. As strong as man is at times, he is rarely stronger than when he has been through the most trying of experiences. On the contrary, a fellow might live in a foreign country and never get the same linguistic level of competence by only hearing and speaking as opposed to studying a language. A mechanic who has worked on cars for twenty years would probably never trade in his experience for a book. Yet, the book-educated mechanics, their managers and employers would probably not trade in their background. The stalemate requires some closing thoughts.

SAMPLE 2

Regardless of the pros and the cons on both sides, not everyone will agree on all the aspects. Character is an individual thing, and every experience is different. Therefore, no two individuals experience the same benefits from the same experience. Likewise, knowledge from a book has the same effect, at least at times, but one tries to get what he can to help him totally develop.

Note to Reader: This is a point-by-point pod. If you lose your thought, you can add a paragraph on defining knowledge, thereby attacking the question.

SAMPLE 3

Essay #3

Question: One argument states that higher education should be open to everyone, regardless of background. The opposing argument says that only the elite students should be allowed to proceed. Discuss these ideas. Do you agree or disagree? Explain why.

Answer pod: 1. Definition 2. Cause-effect

The idea that an education should be available to all or restricted to only good students requires scrutiny on two points. Mainly, the term *good* needs clarification beyond the common idea of better-than-average grades. Plus, the word *open* needs a stricter definition than the normal usage. Let's delve into these ideas.

To insist that students should have an unusually high grade point average to attend college is rooted in the idea that the more motivated students will excel. This is true in many cases. However, the idea of good transcends the stereotype of the guy with thick glasses and his head in a book for six hours every night, in addition to school. The student not taken into consideration here is the one that works for six hours every night in addition to going to school during the day. His grades may be at the B average, but his time is spread more thinly than that of the student who has all As

SAMPLE 3

and has never worked a day in his life. Therefore, the common idea of a good student fails under that light, which leads to the concept of openness.

In many countries now, higher education is available to all students, at least in terms of open enrollment. Nevertheless, *available* does not mean *free*. In the United States, for example, people have the option to attend even if they do not take the high school diploma, but school may not be paid for by the government. Yet, loans are available; there is little excuse not to attend, if a person truly wants to do so. With the right application and the right contacts through government agencies, an aspiring scholar can get that degree. Opportunity is there. There are numerous monies accessible to the public, even in developing countries, such as private grants, private scholarships, federal loans, private loans, and private scholarships, and these are even gotten sometimes by students in developing countries, financed by some of the world's superpowers. Unfortunately, this is not always the case.

The systems are not perfect, and not everyone can live a luxurious life. But the chances are there if people pursue their options. Regardless of what some others may think, we all have to follow our dreams.

Note to Reader: This is a definition pod, with the popular + personal format in the first paragraph. Notice the two definitions for the purpose of two paragraphs in the body.

SAMPLE 4

Essay #4.

Question: Private schools enforce a dress code. Most public schools allow students to dress as they like. Discuss both systems.

Answer pod: 1. Comparison-contrast (paragraph by paragraph) 2. Cause-effect

SAMPLE 4

Allowing a student to express individuality through what he wears has its advantages, but so does wearing a uniform. Personal expression is best at schools that foster individuality. Conversely, a uniform at a military school stresses the need to conform. These ideas require further examination.

Certain schools are built around the idea of nurturing the creative side of a student. Schools like these include performing arts schools, schools for theater, ballet, and even art. To force a child in an environment like one of these to wear a strict kind of clothing would indeed confine one's personal creativity. One's dress is the most basic of personal styles. It speaks volumes about character, class, and color coordination. Performing arts schools are built on the premise that interest should be cultured and refined, even brought out and expressed in public. Therefore, to suppress students' personal styles by imposing a dress code tears down progress in the area of personal expression. On the other hand, expression can sometimes tear down the entire program, as in the military.

Military schools are built on the foundation of obedience. The whole organization runs on orders. The orders come from the top, most often with no explanation at all. The effectiveness of the system is based on the ready compliance of the subordinates to follow the orders. Expression in this kind of environment could have disastrous effects, even death. The purpose is to strip away personal ideas that may conflict with the overall mission of the military as a whole. The dress code might even serve the most basic of functions, such as indicating a student's rank and post. This type of categorizing of the student in school enables the student to be prepared for the real thing in the military, perhaps with the safety of a nation at stake. There is no easy answer to cover all the aspects.

In closing, the dress code, or uniform, holds a very important function in some types of schools, but not in all. In high-crime areas, the uniform is helpful to avoid gang fights brought on by the wearing of certain colors. In private schools, the students know what to expect and readily adopt the uniform. In opposition, other places will never completely accept the idea of the same look, because it goes against the principles of the students and faculty alike.

Essay #5

Question: Colleagues are the people who work with us. In your opinion, what are the qualities of a good colleague? Use specific details and examples in your answer.

Answer pod: 1. Division-classification 2. Definition

The good colleague can be classified into many categories, but the two main categories are apparent. Obviously, the best colleague is a helpful person. Although a good colleague is not always a personal and close friend, he knows how to respect personal space. These ideas necessitate further exploration.

The helpful colleague is there in an infinite number of situations. If one's vehicle is not working satisfactorily, the colleague may offer assistance at the perfect time. A ride goes a long way in the cold. Moreover, the friendly wave from across the room speaks volumes during a long day at work. A watchful eye around the area keeps work overload to a minimum when people help each other out. The needed tool or some advice is sometimes found at the next desk. These things appear small, but they add up. As it is good to see the friend when in need, it is also good not to see him.

Personal space is a luxury that most people cherish. As a result, a worker always wants to see quiet time as quiet time. It can be highly annoying to read something twice. Also, at times, people just do not want to talk. Along those lines, to respect a person's privacy means to know when not to wave, when not to come and ask for a tool, and when not to make conversation. Some final words may shed more light on the subject.

Around the world, people always deal with good and bad coworkers. Regardless of the cultural differences between people, they usually appreciate help and respect. Though the definitions vary, a good colleague is usually helpful and respectful at the same time. It is all a matter of kindness.

Note to Reader: The paper divides the quality of goodness and classifies the examples into (1) helpfulness and (2) respect for personal space. We were given the definition of a colleague in the question, so I did not choose the definition pod.

SAMPLE 6

Essay #6

Question: Do you agree or disagree with the following statement? Participating in sports is worthwhile only when you win something. Use specific reasons and examples to support your answer.

Answer pod: 1. Definition 2. Cause-effect

Participating in sports can certainly be more rewarding if a player wins, but it can be fun even in the face of defeat. The word *only* in the question needs to be examined. In addition, the term *sports* should be defined more clearly. Without looking at these two words more closely, the statement may be illogical.

To deem something effective in a set of circumstances by using the word *only* completely limits its power. Then, the use of *only* here sets up an either-or logical fallacy. In other words, a person can never have fun if he does not win. That suggests that even a ball game with a tied score cannot produce any fun at all. Consequently, during a five-hour game of cricket, not even one minute of fun will be included if the game is lost. The word *only* makes that point unrealistic. There is no way to put off fun until the end of the game and then have it only if one wins. That takes us to the word *game*.

There are countless games in every society on earth. These include athletic games, word games, mind games, and combinations of them all. It is extremely likely that someone will enjoy herself while competing against other people. The nature of many sports reinforces relaxation, laughter, and friendship. Teammates and competitors often joke around during the actual game itself. Adhering to the premise that people have fun only when they win,

SAMPLE 6

it is ridiculous to assume that opponents will even laugh at all until the final score is realized. After all, laughter indicates enjoyment. Furthermore, a lot of games exist whereby one plays against herself. What if she beats herself? Then, who wins and who loses? If she beats her last score, as occurs with many computer games, can she be a happy winner and a sore loser at the same time? These qualifications lead to some final comments.

It is certainly more fun, at least most of the time, to win rather than to lose. However, the sport is in the competition, and the pride is in the excellence. Losing, or not winning the game, is usually a building block to success. Everyone loses at something at some point. The winners learn from it and improve on their mistakes.

Note to Reader: This essay was built on attacking the diction and logic of the question. Always look to the pod of the question and then to the word choice.

SAMPLE 7

Essay #7

Question: Do you agree or disagree with the following statement? Perseverance makes people stronger. Use specific reasons and examples to support your answer.

Answer pod: 1. Cause-effect 2. Division-classification (beneficial vs. nonbeneficial)

Doing things or going through things that are not particularly enjoyable has a world of benefits for the average individual. Immediately, the fortitude produces character. In the long run, things fall into place. At the time, the bothersome task seems worrisome, but it builds strength, leading to self-improvement and a comfortable lifestyle, and eventually a merry heart for what was endured.

Constantly conquering the daily routine establishes an inner strength. This creates a foundation, making everything that is laid

SAMPLE 7

on top seem much easier and more beneficial. The student, for instance, usually does not like to trudge to class on a daily basis with his nose in the books and sit through lecture after lecture. But he does, and it pays off with every little step. Friday's class comes a lot easier than Monday's class comes. The second year is better than the first. The four-hour study session gradually becomes like the two-hour one was before. All in all, the endurance levels increase, both physically and mentally, and the tasks are faced head-on, with a mind-set labeled as character. These immediate benefits have a long-term result, as well.

Over time, from repeatedly doing what one hates to do, for the sake of future success, he starts to reap his harvest from all of the seeds of hard work sown. This may be experienced in a number of ways, namely a better job, more money, a nice house, and vertical mobility. The constant application produces a force that moves problems and barriers. From here, better job offers roll in, all spiraling from the insistence on doing what has to be done, whether enjoyable or not. Corporate professionals in middle management exemplify this principle. They work without stopping, taking every small assignment in stride, until they can finally look back from an angle of repose. But the process does not stop there.

Usually, success at any level will be furthered by completing the necessary menial tasks. At times, the period of reward may seem very distant, but the time of benefit will come, perhaps even gradually. Then, hopefully, one will have the luxury to look back and reflect. Then, he may even say, "I made it."

Note to Reader: The causal chain is the transitional sentence in the introduction.

SAMPLE 8

Essay #8

Question: Do you agree or disagree with the following statement? One should not give up on getting a degree just because she is a little older. Use specific reasons and examples to support your answer.

Answer pod: 1. Definition 2. Cause-effect

An apt rewording of the statement could be that people are never too old to learn. Learning is definitely a lifelong process. A structured environment could very well facilitate the flow of information. These require more discussion.

Whatever the influence, people are always picking up new ideas. This is advantageous for a number of reasons. Primarily, humans look for ways to make things easier, which affects our daily life positively, leaving time for other things like family and relaxation. So, regardless of how people acquire information, it still equals learning. Each time one drives a new way to work in order to save time, he is learning. Similarly, to get things we want, we sometimes have to go through structured programs to get more knowledge on a subject. This, perhaps, may help to get a promotion, receive a higher salary, or even start a new career. Quite a few institutions have recognized this and have planned curricula in response to a growing need.

The advent of the Internet and other outreach programs has caused an explosion in programs for nontraditional university students. Now, more schools than ever before have special programs whereby a student may get a BA, MA, or a PhD without ever attending one class at the university. Our world has become so filled up with other responsibilities that we rarely have the opportunity to attend school, as people did fifty years ago. But diligent school administrators have provided us the luxury of attending school in the comfort of our own homes. The structure of the traditional classroom is not the only one available to meet our needs. The people who were for years looked at sideways for being thirty and returning to school have now supplanted the

SAMPLE 8

focus of programs tailored around their wants and academic needs. New departments have sprung up, or old ones have taken on a new mission. Currently, they include telling names, such as *lifelong learning*, *adult learners*, *nontraditional students*, *distance programs*, *lifelong education*, and many others. The educational institutions are changing with the times.

As technology changes to help us, we will change to better help ourselves. There really are an inordinate number of opportunities to get the education if one wants it badly enough. The population of nontraditional-age students has skyrocketed, so one should never feel out of place. Doing the work is simply a question of priority.

SAMPLE 9

Essay #9

Question: Some people claim living in a rural area is better than living around a lot of people. Comment. Use specific reasons and details to support your answer.

Answer pod: 1. Division-classification 2. Comparison-contrast

People call the city or the small town home for a wealth of reasons, each having its own advantages and disadvantages. Primarily, the small-town people espouse familiarity. In contrast, the city dwellers hide amidst the anonymity. These statements require further scrutiny.

In a small town or in the country, the citizens become acquainted rather quickly. This acquaintance has several subtopics to it. First, families become friends for many generations, and that has a profound impact on lives. The families sometimes intermarry. Consequently, if people do relocate, often they later return to their original home, because both sets of parents live there. Next, land is often involved. Therefore, a kinship is made to the area and not only the people. It is difficult to walk away from an inheritance involving land. Finally, people work together on community projects, bonding them together by the process of building something. If a new Wal-Mart comes to town, everyone feels the spirit of progress together. This stands in direct contrast to life in the city.

The city has many attractive features that lure, just like the small town. The idea of not being readily recognized may appeal to some. With several million people in a metropolis and its surrounding areas, one could go for years and never run into an acquaintance. They probably usually have no desire to return someplace after they leave. There is nothing to keep them stationary. In addition, in that there is no kinship to land, city dwellers like the freedom of mobility. They could move every several months and always have something new. As the city consistently experiences growth, one may look for the best spot to live, replete with post office, an array of restaurants, diversity of culture, and any number of conveniences. The only link a city dweller has in a lot of cases to anything is his own desire to be free. Additional comments follow.

The city and the small town have many benefits to consider. What is right to start out life could change as one gets older. People are lucky at times that they do not have to choose, at least not forever, but can move at will. Maybe this is why some richer people have homes both in the small town and in the city.

Note to Reader: This is a division-classification paper, because we had subtopics in each paragraph. The comparison-contrast paper is better if you actually make a choice. It is our duty to comment on both topics for a complete essay, regardless.

SAMPLE 10

Essay #10.

Question: Snap judgments can never be trusted. Do you agree or disagree with the statement? Use reasons and examples to support your opinion.

Question pod: 1. Cause-effect 2. Definition

Two major types of judgments are usually made quickly. Personal decisions can be catastrophic if made without thinking. On the other hand, professional health care workers are definitely trained to make life-changing decisions every day. The wrong personal decision may lead to heartache just as the wrong professional decision could lead to death.

Decisions involving marriage, family, and significant others can be heartbreaking. Here, if one does not allow time to see the situation from every side, the results might be devastating. These decisions should not be taken lightly. To get married is a prime example. To take this lightly is foolish. The process of deciding takes time and prudence. These are scenarios that do not have life and death hanging in the balance. So, one should avail herself of time available. Unfortunately, for others, especially doctors and nurses, there is no time to sit and think.

One would certainly hope that decisions made quickly are not always wrong. In fact, if that were true, many of our loved ones would not be here with us now. Doctors, namely those in the emergency rooms around the world, are bombarded by situations that require immediate diagnosis and prognosis. If either is wrong, someone may pay with his life. Firemen face danger in the same manner. Rushing into a burning building, turning to the left and to the right, a fireman must absolutely make the right choice, or die. Others depend on him, too. All involved probably know that the stakes are high, any way things go.

The difference between personal and professional decisions is usually twofold. The level of training one has prior to making life decisions and the worst possible result are both inextricably wound up together. It is, then, wise to think in advance. Lastly, it is good that blanket statements do not always ring true.

Note to Reader: This is almost a comparison-contrast pod, but we need to use the cause-effect pod within the structure of the answer and the question itself.

Summary: Answering Test Questions

The following section is from an earlier textbook I wrote for first- and second-year composition classes at the university level. However, I decided to enclose it in this book, because the information is still relevant to the TOEFL exam; the only difference is in the length of the answer. Accordingly, if anything here contradicts earlier information regarding the two-page essay, you should follow the plan given before now and simply think about the strategy of addressing test questions. This information is excellent review material for recognizing cue or key words that indicate the pod required.

A test question can determine the course grade, at times. So, we want to approach this with as much precaution as we possibly can. First, try to find out what type of test you will have, how many points each section is worth, and how that grade figures into your overall course grade.

Essay Question

The essay question is usually an extended paragraph. That is, you should set it up exactly like any paper we have discussed, except you just chop off the introduction and the conclusion. If there is only one essay question on the test, you need to write a complete paper. There may be five to choose from, but you are responsible for only one. The professor usually will give you an idea what exactly to expect in a case like that. Also, time is a factor to take into account when you set up your paper. For example, if you have a two-hour final exam and only one test question, definitely write a full paper. If, however, you must complete four essay questions, write extended paragraphs. Do not let the word *extended* scare you, because such answers are exactly what we have prepared for throughout this text. For the sake of a course test, an extended paragraph should be no less than three-fourths of a handwritten page. That gives you time for four in two hours, or two at two pages each, a good length. With this requirement, condense your examples. Write the points you will address at the top corner of your paper. Go through them in order. You will still have a topic sentence, not a thesis statement, and your evidentiary statements in prescribed order. Then, address them in the order listed at the beginning of the paragraph, just as in any other paper, except, again, we chop off the introduction and the conclusion. Delete the transitional sentences, instead relying on your transitional phrases. If you do not know a point as well as you should, transitional statements should be included, because they provide a certain degree of padding for the paper.

Short-Answer Question

The short-answer question is somewhat tricky in that it may or may not be administered in conjunction with an essay question as described. However, the professor will give you an idea. A short-answer question will usually be worth ten or twenty points. Of course, you will need to gauge the amount of time you have and the amount of writing required to determine how long each answer needs to be. The short-answer question can fool you for that exact reason; however, I always tell my students to remember the acronym CES, which stands for *cause, effect,* and *significance.* Say, for example, tone is a short-answer test question.

Tone—The tone is caused by the diction employed in a written work, which, in turn, was determined by the audience addressed by the piece. The effect of the tone can vary; if the tone is appropriate to the audience (i.e., the reader for which the work was constructed) and the diction conveys the appropriate feeling within the work, the effect will be successful. The significance is that the tone most often signifies the writer's true feelings about the topic on which he writes. (This is worth ten points.)

Tip: If you have ten short-answer questions at five points apiece, limit your answers to three sentences: CES.

Essay Questions

Discuss (CES–Give examples)

Define—See paper pod(s)

Explain (CES–Give examples)

Compare—See paper pod(s)

Compare/contrast—See paper pod(s)

Show how (Explain a procedure by listing the steps in order)

Give examples—See paper pod(s)

Learn to look at the essay questions to determine if the professor/grader gives any indication as to what he wants in your answer. These are the most common cue words in essay questions, but they are so broad that there is often something else in the question that should tip you off.

Example Questions

Discuss

Discuss the importance of exercise to the cardiovascular system.

This question tells me that the professor/grader wants the CES approach. This is so general that you must write all you know. Importance is the same as significance. Also, the question specifies "to the cardiovascular system." That means he wants the effect.

Define

This has two parts: the popular and the personal. The personal is not your idea, but it is the professor's idea about something. If the professor says, "I think . . . ," write it down, and put three stars by what he said. This is most likely a test question in formation. You can also write, "According to the book . . ."

Explain

Explain and *discuss* basically are the same thing. However, another key word generally comes after *explain,* such as "explain the relevance." Then, talk about connections in works, ideas, and examples.

Compare

Think about the comparison-contrast pod talked about earlier. Set it up according to how much time you have and the points for each test question. Do not stray too far from the pod(s) given previously.

Give Examples

Move back and forth from generalities to specifics. Support what you say through concrete examples. This is the perfect place to include the partial quotes mentioned earlier. When you cannot remember a particular quote, it is easy to throw in some key words you memorized from your notes or the book. If you have not remembered any definitions from your readings, you need to use your weapon—your pen—more frequently during study.

Cue Words

These are words that help you determine what pod to employ in essay answers.

Cause-effect: *leads to, result, starts, reason, cause,* and *consequence.*

Comparison-contrast: *difference, similarities, in common, alike,* and *same.*

Definition-describe: *tell about, name, most people say, termed, deemed, called, labeled,* and *represented as.*

Explication

This means to take a line or quote out of a statement and to explain its relevance to the structure as a whole. To do this, you must rely on the importance of the statement in reference to the complete statement. Nevertheless, think CES. Also, the quote may be indicative of a theme that has run throughout the piece. To do this, you want to target any sort of qualifiers that may be included, such as *always, maybe, never, seems, appears, suggests,* and so on. If so, set up the paper with your ES(s) and write accordingly. See example below.

SAMPLE

Passage:

**Everything moves in circles.** The smaller circle moves in epicycles. They move around a bigger circle. The bigger ones are even part of a huge chain, with a small overlap, each sharing a common piece. Therefore, they are wrapped up in one another.

Test Question: Some people say that "everything moves in circles." Do you agree or disagree with that statement? Give examples to support your ideas.

Remember: I said earlier that you must always think of yourself as being in the paper that you write. Look at yourself geographically. Look at the sentence that we must explicate.

Sample Explication:

The sentence seems to be relevant to the text in the language employed and the position of the statement in the text. The statement blatantly declares that "everything" is connected. Consequently, there is absolutely no room for any refutation to the contrary. This, in turn, leads to the statement's position in the text. By asserting this idea at the beginning, the writer has laid the groundwork for his entire argument. He continues this pattern by explaining how "smaller" circles move around bigger circles, which also move in a "big chain." The diction exercised suggests that all is hooked together, expounding on the original claim that "everything" is linked with a "small overlap." His final statement adds the finale to his short claim, saying that all is "wrapped up." Therefore, the writer has used the quote as a starting place on which to build his entire argument, adding to it link by link, statement by statement, moving from the smaller example to the larger with each assertion.

NOTE:

There were no value judgments applied to the explicatory statement, no condemnation, only a reaction to the structure of his paper. The whole reaction written in the explication focused on only structure and diction in the piece reviewed. The two were ample to address the question and write a piece in reaction to it.

Wrapping everything up, I must stress again that the essays are a series of hoops to jump through, each one making you stronger, so much so that you can fly through your academic career with what you have learned thus far. If you have any questions concerning writing, look back at your pods. They are designed to be changed according to specific questions and audiences. You can do well. Good luck.

Additional Grammar Rules

Participles

Participles: -ed, -ing; in order to; for; as well as vs. *as well; neither/nor; either* vs. *neither; so, also, too;* gerunds, infinitives.

<u>How do I know when to use *-ing* or *-ed* on the end of a word?</u>

NOTE: *We are referring to words used as adjectives. Remember: These are verbals, forms of verbs that are used as adjectives, and here they are adjectivals. Refer to Syntactical Structures if you have questions.*

We can use these in the transformation from active voice to passive voice to determine the form of the word that should be employed. The parts of the sentences are labeled below the words. For example, the word *me* is the DO in the first sentence, indicated as such by the abbreviation DO below it. See the glossary for any abbreviations you can't remember.

Examples:

Confusing/ Confused

Active Sentence:

Grammar confuses me. (Simple Present)

S–V–DO

Grammar is confusing me.

S–aux–MV–DO (The verb is pres. prog.)

NOTE: *The -ing causes the action, so it turns into the adjective in the second passive sentence. (CAUSE)*

Grammar will confuse me.

S–aux.–MV–DO (Simple Future)

Passive Sentence:

Therefore, I am confused by grammar.

S–Aux–Verb 3 (v3) + by obj.

 **NOTE:** *The -ed receives the action, so it is the adjective in the first passive sentence. (EFFECT)*

Effect

Therefore, grammar is confusing.

(Confusing = Adjective)

S–LV–SC/adj/verbal

Various Verbs:

Passive:

I was confused.

I was being confused.

I will be confused.

Complement Construction: The adjectives in these sentences are only subject complements, not verbs. If a noun is placed behind them, they become action verbs. This is why they are so difficult to learn.

It is confusing.

It was confusing.

It will be confusing.

Remember: **The *-ing* word is the *cause*** with an object, and if we drop the object, we know that word is used to describe a noun that causes a feeling. **The *-ed* word receives the *effect*** from the *-ing* word. See below.

Boring: The theater is boring me.

Therefore, it is boring.

Bored: I am being bored by the theater.

I am bored.

Interesting: The movie is interesting the people.

Therefore, it is interesting.

Interested: The people are being interested by the movie.

Therefore, they are interested.

Stunning: The woman is stunning me.

Therefore, she is stunning.

Stunned: I am being stunned by the woman.

Therefore, I am stunned.

Astounding: The method was astounding me.

Therefore, the method was astounding.

Astounded: I was being astounded by the method.

Therefore, I was astounded.

You can change the tenses with these verbs. However, some words will not take the adjectival form in the past participle, nor will they take an active pattern.

Ex: She is cunning. Not: I was being cunned.

He is sympathizing. Not: I was sympathized. (Needs prep. with)

Other words that follow this pattern:

Exhilarating, exhilarated

Incapacitating, incapacitated

Debilitating, debilitated

Enthralling, enthralled

Striking, stricken

Entrancing, entranced

Inspiring, inspired

Enhancing, enhanced (with things, usually)

Overwhelming, overwhelmed

Intoxicating, intoxicated

Surprising, surprised

Stifling, stifled

Shocking, shocked

Frustrating, frustrated

Judging, judged

Condemning, condemned

Liberating, liberated

Tempting, tempted

In Order To, To: Ellipsis & Relocating in a Sentence:

In order to indicates reason; it answers the question, why?

This is alluded to under infinitive of reason in the Grammar section.
The following sentences carry the same meaning:

Sam went there in order to buy some bread.

Sam went there to buy some bread.

We come here in order to learn a different language.

We come here to learn a different language.

We said earlier that an infinitive of reason is to + verb 1 (v1). All we did was take out the words in order. As a result, what remains is to + v1. The first verb immediately after to is almost always base form, referred to as v1. The infinitive of reason can be repositioned in the sentence and continue to function in the same capacity. Here again, this is the common denominator in most of the structures we have learned so far. There always seems to be another possibility in the positioning of a phrase or clause in the sentence. Note the patterns that emerge below as we analyze the possibilities.

Syntactic positions: Initial = at the beginning of the sentence

Final = at the end of the IC.

Initial:

In order to learn, we study daily.

To learn, we study daily.

In order to be there on time, we must leave early.

To be there on time, we must leave early.

In order to study the material successfully, you must take organized notes.

To study the material successfully, you must take organized notes.

The first verb after the word to *is the first form (v1) in all of the sentences. This is true even if the verb is five words after* to. *If you include the first part of the phrase* in order, *it is still necessary to use v1 after the word* to. *We only omit* in order.

Final

I went to the store <u>in order to</u> shop.

I went to the store <u>to shop.</u>

We turned off the radio <u>in order to</u> sleep better.

We turned off the radio __to sleep__ better.

I am here __in order to__ set things straight.

I am here __to set__ things straight.

> ### NOTE:
>
> *We can add an object to many of these patterns.*

To see the game, we went higher.

To buy the car, I worked more hours.

I saved room to eat dessert.

I practiced more to run the race.

To understand a person, you must try. (Can be moved to DO in final position)

One should read more to know his history.

I encouraged him more to benefit myself.

To win the race, we trained harder.

> ### NOTE:
>
> *These are usually, but not always, interchangeable from final to initial positions, and vice versa.*

For: The Use of For as Reason: Syntactic Repositioning

Earlier, we viewed *for* in respect to use with a gerund functioning to signal reason in a sentence.

Pattern: IC = S–V + (optional) + *For* + Gerund

Ex: We are only here __for learning.__

I go there daily __for relaxing.__

He uses it __for exercising.__

It is possible to use *for* in the same sentence construction with the use of a noun. However, in the following sentences, we can replace the word *for* with the phrase *to get*, and the meaning does not change. The implication in each of these sentences then is that the subject performs an action to receive something in return.

Pattern: IC = S–V + (optional) + *For* + Noun

Ex: I went to the store for bread.

He went to the hospital for a checkup.

I work here for (the) money.

I walked to town for cigarettes.

He stopped for fuel.

He goes there for (the) admiration.

But, in the next few sentences, the subject is doing something without a tangible benefit. In other words, the subject is simply performing an action, but not for bread, cigarettes, money, and so on.

I go to church for prayer. (Can mean "to pray" or "to receive prayer")

I went there for penance.

I attend the service for confession.

He goes there for mass.

Also, these above are not appropriate in the initial position. Additionally, it is acceptable to indicate a holiday, festival, or celebration with *for* + noun.

He went for Easter.

He left for Christmas.

He stays for his birthday.

I always prepare for New Year's Day.

So = Cause/Effect: Syntactic Repositioning

For the most part, it is easy to view a sentence with the word *so*, if it contains two different clauses, in terms of cause and effect.

Cause/*so*/Effect

The first clause is the cause, and the second clause is the effect.

> I want to be trim, so I exercise every day.
>
> I needed a haircut, so I went to the barber.
>
> We should have been home at 8:00, so we're leaving right now.
>
> We were very tired, so we went to bed early.

Effect/*so*/Cause

It is possible to invert most of these structures with *so*, adding the word *because* and replacing the modal. The second clause tells why the first clause happened. The second clause, consequently, is the reason the first clause took place.

> We arrived extremely early, so we could surprise my friend.
>
> I sought out the best teachers, so I could learn Arabic.
>
> I called John, so he would bring my books.
>
> We went to the sea, so we could relax.

Effect/*Because*/S–V

It is common to replace the *so* with the word *because*, which actually means *the cause is . . .*

Sometimes, it's mandatory to change the wording for the sentence to be grammatical. Compare the sentence patterns with what we have discussed so far.

> We arrived extremely early, because we wanted to surprise my friend.
>
> We got our coats, because it became cold.
>
> We were angry, because they were not nice.

We got up early, so we could go to the park.

We woke up earlier, because we were going to the lake.

So we could go to the lake, we got up early.

Because we were going home, we arose earlier than usual.

NOTE: *Do not use* because *and* so *in the same superstructure if there are only two clauses.*

So and *because* can be subordinators when placed in the initial position syntactically, thereby making an IC dependent.

IC

Because I was impatient, <u>I called the man myself</u>.

Sub.

So I can get more sleep, I go to bed at 9:00.

Sub.

However, *so* and *because* can also be conjunctive adverbs (CA).

I went to the store. <u>So</u>, she went, too. (Therefore)

Why are you eating? <u>Because, I am hungry</u>.

In both sets of sentences, the conjunctive adverbs link the ideas between the ICs. If these conjunctive adverbs are linking two ICs into one giant sentence (superstructure), they are c/cs. See the chapters on punctuation and transitions. Commas must offset these, or else they make the IC a sentence fragment.

So, Also, Too, As Well, As Well As

These adverbs indicate agreement. Look over the following patterns.

I went to the store, and so did he.

S–V (+) V–S (+)

He ran, so did I.

S–V (+) V–V (+)

I am a man, and he is, also.

S–LV–SC (+) S–V (+)

He practices the guitar, and Jim does, also.

S–V (+) S–V (+)

He teaches at the university, and I also teach there.

S–V (+) S–V (+)

I cleaned the car. Also, I washed the clothes.

S–V (+) CA S–V (+)

The position of *also* is usually mobile. Generally, it may be present in the initial, medial, and final positions.

He goes to New York, and I do, too.

S–V (+) S–V (+)

Dick collects cards, and I too collect them. (Comma optional)

S–V (+) S–V (+)

No initial positioning allowed.

I attended the wedding. Rod went, as well.

S–V (+) S–V (+)

They want peace. I, as well, want peace.

S–V (+) S–V (+)

Medial and final positions are common.
As well as means *in addition to* (*and*).

He ordered chicken as well as turkey at the restaurant.

S–V N–*as well as*–N

She is smart as well as pretty.

S–V–Adj.–*as well as*–Adj.

He runs fast as well as hard.

S–V–Adv.–*as well as*–Adv.

The patterns are clear, because there is often no interference between the word before *as well as* and the word immediately thereafter, which indicates the coordination. The patterns do, however, vary, but, for the most part, these stand out.

As Well As

N, Adj, Adv, V
Patterns:
S–V–N–*as well as*–N

I got a shirt as well as a hat.

I received a broken arm as well as a cracked rib.

She bought a car as well as a boat.

S–V–Adj.–*as well as*–Adj.

That man is kind as well as rich.

She is shy as well as motivated.

She is quick on her feet as well as fast with her serve.

S–V–Adv.–*as well as*–Adv.

He ran the campaign effectively as well as cheaply.

He addressed the public halfheartedly as well as cunningly.

The boy answered respectfully as well as quickly.

S–V–*as well as*–V

He runs as well as lifts weights.

She dances as well as sings.

He lies as well as steals.

Combining an adjective with a noun or creating some other combination is not a problem, as long as the construction is grammatical. The components of the sentence must agree with the verb. It may be necessary to add something.

She is pretty as well as a good athlete.

He is running daily as well as maintaining his agenda.

Either, Neither, Nor

I do not like tea, and he doesn't either.

S–V (−) S–V (−)

I haven't eaten, and he hasn't either.

S–V (−) S–V (−)

We won't see it, and you won't either.

S–V (−) S–V (−)

We are not coming, and neither are they.

S–V (−) V–S (+)

The word *neither* is a negative in and of itself, because it is a contraction of *either* and *not*, but we will call the second clause positive to remember the patterns more easily.

They didn't arrive and neither did the luggage.

S–V (−) V–S (+)

Nor takes the same pattern as *neither*.

I do not drink nor does my wife.

S–V (−) V–S (+)

I will not listen, nor will I indulge the thought.

S–V (−) V–S (+)

Think of *nor* as a contraction of *not* and *or*, so it is inherently negative like *neither*.

PART II:
Grammar

CHAPTER FOUR

Parts of Speech

Parts of Speech

Nouns

A noun is the name of a (1) person, (2) place, or (3) thing. Nouns are either proper or common. For example, the name of a person is a proper noun. So, when we write the name *Tom Smith*, it should be capitalized. However, the word *boy* does not require capitalization. It is a **common noun.**

The name of a specific place, such as New York, requires capitalization. It is a certain place, and there is only one New York City at that exact location. However, a location like the mountains is the name of a place, but there are many mountains, and one must be specific in order to make this a **proper noun.** A thing may describe an infinite number of possibilities; therefore, most things come under the heading of common nouns, which generally do not need to take a capital letter. These are some good examples: *car, ship, house,* and *computer.* Note that if we put a specific name to the noun, we must capitalize it. For example, *Lexus, Titanic,* and *Alpha* are all good examples of very specific nouns that require capitalization. So, we see that there are *proper nouns* and *common nouns.* Proper nouns take capital letters, and common nouns do not.

NOTE: *One must always capitalize* Far East, Middle East, Near East, North America, South America, Europe, *and* Asia.

There is also a set of nouns that we call <u>*abstract.*</u> These nouns name items that are not tangible. One cannot touch them or hold them in his hand. Arguably, they can be felt. A good example is *grief.* One can certainly feel the death of a family member, but the feeling is abstract, untouchable. *Happiness, sadness, excitement, danger,* and *anxiety* are all abstract nouns, and they are not written with capital letters.

Concrete nouns, on the other hand, can be touched. Some examples are *pennies, paper, water,* and *cups.* They are either count or noncount as seen below.

Count nouns are those that can be physically counted; in other words, one can see the number of the things at hand, or, better put, in hand. *Boys, girls, cigarettes, rocks,* and *fingers* are all count nouns. If you can put an *s* on the end of the word, it is probably a count noun.

Noncount nouns are those that cannot be counted. Perhaps it is not impossible, at least sometimes, to count some of these nouns we call noncount, but it is unlikely that one would try to count these types of nouns. *Sugar, sand,* and *hair* are noncount nouns. Further, *water, tea,* and *cream* are what we would call uncountable, which seems more appropriate.

NOTE: *If we say something like "I had two cups of tea," then we can number the actual cups, but not the tea itself.*

Usage Note: *people, money, food.*

Exercise 4.1

Directions: Label the nouns in each sentence, indicating *C* for *count*, *NC* for *noncount*, *CM* for *common*, and *P* for *proper*. In addition, capitalize any proper nouns. The answers are always on top when labeling is required.

C/CM

1. We went to the store.
2. There were bubbles in the water.
3. I had 500 bottles of air.
4. We will have the beef.
5. Whoever said it was wrong.
6. We found a note.
7. The herb was safe.
8. The safety of the men was the issue.
9. Along the way, we went to the statue of liberty.
10. The Midwest was rainy on Thursday.
11. The money earmarked for the interstate highway commission was misappropriated.
12. Different coffees from around the world provided us quite a variety.
13. The continental divide is a famous tourist attraction.
14. If the manager had known, he would have closed early.
15. At the mall, the angry crowd burned the postal truck.
16. The united states post office is extremely efficient.
17. The girl from micronesia swam very well.
18. School can be rewarding.
19. Religion has been the cornerstone of many people's lives.
20. Snobbishness is a bad characteristic.
21. Accuracy is necessary in grammar.
22. Being lazy is an unfavorable trait.
23. The desert is extremely hot.
24. If dinosaurs were in this spot a million years ago, we would now have evidence.
25. Trust is paramount to a good relationship between family members.
26. Some say that the horse became expendable with the advent of the modern car.

27. The germanic languages have similar sentence patterns to English.
28. He said history is his favorite subject.
29. I said that american history from 1865 to world war I is my favorite course.
30. Ode to a grecian urn is the name of a poem.

Verbs

Verbs are a little more complicated than most of the other parts of speech. We will be concerned with several different kinds of verbs here.

Be Verbs

Be verbs are so called because they are conjugations of the verb *be*. They include the following: (1) simple present: *is, am, are*; (2) simple past: *was, were*; (3) simple future: *will* (*be*)

We will finish the tenses in the next few pages under "Action Verbs."

From these three tenses, one can form many different tenses of action. *Tense* refers to the time of an occurrence. Let's look at the *be* verbs and the persons that go with them. *Person* means the pronoun/name used with the verb.

Look at the list below and the pronouns used with each.

Simple Present:	Simple Past	Simple Future
I am.	I was.	I, you, he, she, it, they, we + will be
You are.	You were.	
We are.	We were.	
They are.	They were.	
He is.	He was.	
She is.	She was.	
It is.	It was.	

These are only the most simple verb forms. Verbs basically have several functions. First, we need to look at the different classes of verbs before we are able to go into any detail on their functions.

The verbs above are the only verbs in the sentence, but they are really not doing anything. **One could say that they point out a state of existence.** That is precisely what a *be* verb does when it is the only verb in the sentence. Let's look at some examples.

I am a man.

Now, when I look at that sentence, I think that there are only a few kinds of words that I could possibly put in place of the word *man.* Believe me, I have heard that sentence many times from my two young boys. I usually reply or answer with, "No, you are a boy, a puppy, a mouse," or something equally as clever. I always remember that the word after the *be* verb, sometimes called a linking verb, is telling me something about the noun before the *be* verb.

Logic:

We could say, "I am nice." The words *nice* and *man* describe (tell about) the word *man.* However, there is no action performed by anyone or anything. It is inactive. We call this a ***stative*** verb. It seems to indicate a state of existence that the subject is in, either temporarily or permanently. However, I can put a phrase, a word, or a group of words after the *be* verb that tells where the subject is. For instance, "I am at my house." The words after *am* tell where I am located. They do not describe the word *I,* but they do not show any action either. Therefore, a *be* verb alone in a sentence is called a stative verb, indicating something about the subject's state of existence. This means that there is a limit on the types of words that are allowed after a *be* verb.

Tip: The easiest way to remember the *be* verb is like this: Be nice! Be good! Be a man! The commands tell the person what or how to be; therefore, the verb is a *be* verb. Note the answer: I will be!

Linking Verbs: Two Types

Be Verbs

The *be* verbs here simply tie the subject to its complement. The complement renames, completes, or describes the subject. A noun, adjective, or a verb/other word acting like an adjective realizes the complement.

S–LV–SC (subject complement)

Noun: The boy is a student.

The girl is my friend.

The cat is a winner.

S–LV–SC

Adjective: The dog is wild.

The man was angry.

Our party will be the best.

S–LV–SC

Verb: He is tired.

I became worn-out.

The man was shattered.

 **NOTE:** *The linking verb and the* be *verb are really the same thing, but if we keep them separated as they are now, we will avoid confusion with complements that are realized by nouns rather than adjectives. Look at these:*

Stay calm! Stay is a *be* verb.

Compare the sentence above to the one below.

The man was shattered. *Was* is a *be* verb, but if we remember it as a linking verb, we know that *shattered* is an adjective, but we would never command someone to be shattered (sad or brokenhearted). Therefore, although the distinction seems small at first, you will need to know it for sentence structure.

Copula Verbs: *Seem, Appear, Feel, Look, Acted, Remain, Sound*

These basically act the same as linking verbs in some contexts, although *appear, feel, look, act,* and *sound* can also be action verbs. Here, the verbs are all copulas with a complement to the right that describes the subject.

Caution: If the word after the verb does not rename or tell about the subject, you probably have an action verb and not a copula. Example: He appeared suddenly. *Suddenly* describes how he appeared and not him.

He felt lonely.

She appeared happy.

The child felt sad when his father left.

I looked stupid.

We acted like real monsters.

He remained calm during the crisis.

They sound very genuine.

The biggest class of verbs is the action verb. The action verb is in essence the opposite of a *be* verb. If we think of the action verb like this, learning the grammar of English will be much easier.

 **NOTE:** *Learning a language can be difficult, but if you learn the verbs and how they work in the structure, you are on the way to success. This is even true in learning the vocabulary.*

The action verb is used to convey or give information on an action that is done, was done, is being done now, or will be done at some time in the future. Action verbs can have helping verbs (depending on the tense), or they can function alone. The helpers of action verbs in a sentence are always *be* verbs or helping verbs—that is, *has, have,* and *had* ("perfect" helping verbs).

I was walking to the market.

I have been walking to and from the market all day.

This sentence tells me that the action was occurring for a certain amount of time in the past. We can add to the main verb, the action verb, and change the time at which this walking happened or will happen. A verb paradigm, or verb list with the different tenses, is what we need to view now.

Present Progressive	**Past Progressive**
I am walking.	I was eating.
He is walking.	He was singing.
She is walking.	She was talking.
It is walking.	It was sleeping.
They are walking.	They were eating.
We are walking.	We were answering the questions.
You are walking.	You were running.
Future Progressive	**Simple Future**
I will be walking.	I will walk.
He will be singing.	He will sing.
She will be talking.	He will sing.
It will be eating.	It will eat.
They will be answering the questions.	They will answer.
You will be running.	You will run.

Verb Tenses

Compare the forms of the verbs. The **simple past** means that the action happened, and now it is over. It occurred as a simple incident, probably only once. The action was not happening again and again. However, one can say, "I smoked from 1995 to 1996." It happened for one year, but it is viewed as a completed action.

In the progressive tense, sometimes called the continuous, the action of the verb occurs progressively for a duration of time, or it takes place (present progressive) for a duration of time usually specified by a time tag. For example, *I was eating from 8:00 until 9:00* means that I was busy performing that action for one hour. The meaning is the same in the future and present progressive forms. However, there are certain times when we use the present progressive to indicate that we will do something in the future. This is most commonly used with the expression *am going to. I am going to the store at 5:00* describes a future action if the person says this at 3:00 in the afternoon. This is colloquial, not commonly used in writing; rather, it should not be used in academic writing. It is certainly informal.

Simple future means that the action will take place later, and it will happen only for that minute or specific time, not in a continuing manner like the progressive.

Here, we need to make a distinction between the simple present and the progressive. The simple present indicates that the action takes place over and over, but, unlike the progressive, the action is not for a specific period of time. The progressive has a limit on the duration of time, even if this means that the time limit is not known exactly. A good simple present is this: *I eat fruit.* Now, of course, we do not know exactly when, but the verb suggests that the action occurs frequently. However, this person does not eat all day and all night. That would be impossible. *I am eating fruit* indicates that the action is taking place at this very minute. Usually, there is a time tag (a word or words that tell exactly when).

Tip: Always look for a time tag in a sentence, in addition to the verb phrase. Always do this when working with the progressive tense. If you are writing a paper, include time tags; also, the progressive tense usually indicates that an action is performed continually–not continuously. That means the speaker or the subject enjoys brief periods of cessation (stopping) in the activity.

I was coming <u>at 6:00</u>. Now I am not.

I was going <u>at 7:00</u>. Now I am not.

We were riding <u>on Tuesday</u>. But we changed plans.

I will be leaving <u>at 4:00</u>.

I will be going <u>on Fridays</u>.

I will be going to the store. (No time tag.)

The girl was making candy tomorrow, but now she has decided not to make it.

Perfect Forms

The perfect forms are usually what most students have problems with when studying English, even the best students. Because of this, we will view a timeline to simplify things.

_____Past Perfect_____Simple Past_____Now *Had* + verb 3 X *Has* + verb_3_____−*

Completed

The past perfect verb consists of the verb *had* + the third form of a verb. To make this clear, we will look at a regular verb (one that takes *-ed* in the simple past tense) and an irregular verb (one that does not take *-ed* in the simple past tense).

NOTE: *Hereafter, we will call the* be *verbs auxiliary verbs when they accompany other verbs, specifically if they come before another verb in a sentence. The function of these auxiliary verbs is to help the main verb, the action verb, form a grammatical and therefore logical sentence.*

Past Perfect

Always supposes we can put the word *before* in the sentence.

Had + v3 (third form of verb)

I <u>had walked</u> to the store *the day before yesterday.*

I <u>had eaten</u> dinner *before I went to the restaurant.*

The verb phrase *had walked* took place before some time in the simple past. Here, the simple past was *yesterday.*

Similarly, the verb phrase *had eaten* happened before some time in the simple past, which was *I went to the restaurant.*

In both sentences, the action took place and was completed entirely before some time in the past. Be aware that the italicized phrases will be called time tags when examining sentences in the future. Now, we know that these actions are already completed. With the present perfect, it is not so easy to discern exactly when the action was completed. With the perfect tenses—and we will look at a third next—the action is completed before a fixed time; with present perfect, the fixed time is *now.*

Present Perfect

Has/Have + v3

I have watched television (until/before).

This indicates that I have watched the television at a time before or until now. The fixed time in the present perfect is always now.

Future Perfect

Will/Shall + *have* + v3

I will have watched the movie *by 9:00.*

I shall have played basketball *by Tuesday.*

 **NOTE:** Shall *is British English, used mostly in the United Kingdom and parts of Asia.* Shall *basically means that the situation is imperative (an order). It is not unacceptable in the United States, but it is highly uncommon. Hereafter, British English will be abbreviated as Br.E.*

Also, note the time tag at the end of the sentence in the form of by + noun or a time phrase.

Tip: Remember: *Had always* = past tense.

Have/has always = present tense.

Verb Conjugation: Past Tenses

When reference is made to v3, the conjugation is as follows. Regular verbs are formed by adding *-ed* to the base to form the simple past tense. The simple past, however, has no helping verb in an active sentence (i.e., one in which the subject does the action). In the past perfect, the same method is used as in the simple past tense, but the auxiliary verb *had* is situated prior to the main verb and even prior to the helping verb in a verb phrase with three words (i.e., *had been walking*). Likewise, the auxiliary *had* is also used before irregular verbs that do not take *-ed* to form the simple past tense, if the tense is the perfect (i.e., *he had lent the boy some money*). Most students make errors with the irregular verbs, because they have not memorized them. We call these verbs in the perfect tenses third form, or v3. A new word, at least in appearance, is formed in the irregular verbs by a process called gradation, or ablaut, wherein the internal vowels change (e.g., *stuck*, *wrote*, *broke*). This third form, as we call it, is even usually different from the simple past tense, or the preterite. Thus, a new form must be learned by rote (i.e., practicing again and again). Refer to the irregular verb list.

Exercise 4.2

Directions: Fill in correct form of the verb tense.

1. I_____(go) to the store before I saw you yesterday.
2. We will have_____(complete) the form by the end of the day.
3. I will have_____ (see) you by the time I leave.
4. _____(had, have, has) you eaten before you came?
5. I saw you when you were_____(come) down the hill.
6. Who_____(tell) you that I was here?
7. Before I saw him, he had_____(come) here.
8. If I had (know)_____, I would have arrived earlier.
9. Can you (see)_____if I move?
10. If I were (walk)_____, I would not have my keys in my hand.
11. If I had (see)_____the dog, I would tell you.
12. As you run, I will be _____(run) with you.
13. As most people _____(know) already, we will be (learn) _____more as time goes by.
14. She (walk)_____yesterday, but I had_____(go) before then.
15. If he is (go)_____to the post office later, _____(give) him this letter, please.
16. Because they had (break up)_____their companies, the competitors _____(get) most of the profits.

17. What I (want)_____to see was the success of all of the students.
18. Although I had not (see)_____him, I_____(know) then that he was in town.
19. Because they were (go)_____ so slowly, the meteor _____(overtake) them in a matter of seconds.
20. After you (give)_____me the green light, I (send)_____your letter to the boss.
21. What bothers me is that as you are (get up)_____, I will be (go)_____to bed.
22. Not knowing the truth is what had (give)_____me the problem before you finally (tell)_____me.
23. I had_____(lend) him money far in advance.
24. Too much responsibility always (cause)_____problems with irresponsible tenants.
25. Since you will be (arrive) _____early, could I (impose)_____ on you for a ride?

Exercise 4.3

Directions: Write *C* for *copula verb* or *A* for *action verb* for the underlined words.

1. He sounded the bell loudly due to the impending storm.
2. He looked tired after being on the road for two days.
3. As we walked through the pyramids, a rainbow appeared over the horizon.
4. It seemed as if we were lost.
5. He reacted calmly.
6. We remained calm through the night
7. Something smelled fishy about his late-night meetings.
8. He smelled badly, because his nose was broken.
9. I felt bad about having her dog put outside.
10. He appears to know what he is doing.
11. The paper felt rough.

EXERCISE 4.3

12. He looked about the room furtively.
13. He acted tough.
14. He acted very obnoxiously at dinner.
15. We wanted to ensure that the room did not smell bad.
16. He was acting like a security guard.
17. They remained in the ambulance.
18. The excuse sounded like a lie.

Modal Verbs

Can, could, may, might, shall, should, will, would, must, ought to, need, and dare.

Rule: Syntactically (in a sentence), the very first verb following the modal must always be the base form, uninflected, what we refer to as verbal, even if it is an auxiliary verb.

Functions

Modals express mood: indicative, subjunctive, and imperative.

<u>Indicative</u>—objective fact

<u>Imperative</u>—command, order, obligation

<u>Subjunctive</u>—expresses a contingent or hypothetical action

Although we say that some of these verbs are the past tense of other forms, they do not necessarily function in that manner. Let's define them; then we will rank them.

Expression	Modal	Example
Future	will	I will eat less.
Ability	can/could	I can go home. I could go home if . . .
Ability (past)	could	I could swim when I was eight.
Necessity	must/have	I must protect my children. I have to work.

Advisability	should/had better	You should stop smoking. You had better . . .
Possibility	may/might	I may return. I might go home.
Permission	may/might/ can/could	May I leave now? (Formal)
Conditional	may, might, would, could, will + if	

The base form of a verb always follows modal verbs, perhaps not immediately thereafter, but the next verb is always base form. *Had better* is colloquial. **The rules of formality should be applied in written assignments, but, in conversation, most of these are interchangeable.** To understand the differences between the modals, we need to rank them according to the possible result if a requirement is not met. This is simply a rough guideline to follow for some of the modal verbs.

Modal	**Result**	
Must/Have	Bodily injury, terrible penalty	I must protect my family.
Should/Had better	Terrible penalty– perhaps delayed	I should study more. / I ought to study more.

NOTE: *Must can also be used with logical alternatives, which means that one comes to a conclusion based on the evidence at hand. Ex: His car is there, so he must be at home. This usage indicates likelihood or probability.*

Exercise 4.4

Directions: Choose the appropriate answer.

1. The little boy is late. He _____get home before his mother becomes angry. (ought to, had better, can, must)
2. I really _____start exercising more, because I want to look good for my reunion. (must, should, could, would)
3. _____I actually register my car? (must, should, can, had better)
4. _____you let me borrow your pen? (should, could, may)
5. The boy said, "Do I _____wear this tie?" (need, must, have to, better)
6. You_____have the doctor check you over every year. (must, should, need, might)
7. Everyone_____eat a balanced diet, although most do not. (must, shall, might, ought to, may)
8. I_____go to the movie if I had enough money. (can, should, will, would)
9. _____a teacher allow the students to cheat on a test? (can, could, should, must)
10. The man thought he _____ (could, would, will, can) have fame and glory if he _____ (shall, will, would, could, might) only get to the top of the mountain.

Answers to Exercise 4.1

Directions: Label the nouns in each sentence, indicating *C* for *count*, *NC* for *noncount*, *CM* for *common*, and *P* for *proper*. In addition, capitalize any proper nouns. The answers are always on top when labeling is required.

       C/CM
1. We went to the store.

       C/CM   NC/CM
2. There were bubbles in the water.

       C/CM   NC/CM
3. I had 500 bottles of air.

NC/CM

4. We will have the beef.

      C/CM

5. Whoever said it was wrong. Plural of *it* = *they* (subj.)/*them* (obj.)

      C/CM

6. We found a note.

      C/CM

7. The herb was safe.

      NC/C C/CM   C/CM

8. The safety of the men was the issue.

      C/CM   C/P

9. Along the way, we went the Statue of Liberty. Liberty is C or NC.

      NC/P   C/P

10. The Midwest was rainy on Thursday.

     C or NC/CM   C/P

11. The money earmarked for the Interstate Highway Commission was misappropriated.

      C or NC/CM   C/CM C/CM

12. Different coffees from around the world provided us quite a variety. Note: *Coffee, people*, and *money* are NC unless one specifies different origins or varieties.

      C/P   C/CM

13. The Continental Divide is a famous tourist attraction. Note: The nouns referred to in numbers 9, 11, and 13 are considered NC if there is only one of that specific proper noun, but, of course, there can be many statues, highways, and divides, at which point, separately, they are common and countable.

      C/CM

14. If the manager had known, he would have closed early.

      C/CM   C/CM   C/CM

15. At the mall, the angry crowd burned the postal truck.

      C/P

16. The United States Post Office is extremely efficient. See note in number 13. Here, we can pluralize *office*, so it becomes countable, unless we specify the institution as a whole.

    C/CM   C/P

17. The girl from Micronesia swam very well. Micronesia is an area made up of many islands; therefore, we must follow the rule set forth for regions (i.e., the Middle East).
    C/CM

18. School can be rewarding.
    C/CM C/CM C or NC/CM C/CM

19. Religion has been the cornerstone of many people's lives. See note in number 12.
    NC/CM   C/CM

20. Snobbishness is a bad characteristic.
    NC/CM C or NC/CM

21. Accuracy is necessary in grammar. Grammar is NC if one does not specify types.
    C/CM

22. Being lazy is an unfavorable trait.
    C/CM

23. The desert is extremely hot.
    C/CM C/CM C/CM

24. If dinosaurs were in this spot a million years ago, we would know.
   NC/CM C/CM C/CM

25. Trust is paramount to a good relationship between family members.
    NC/CM   C/CM NC/CM C/CM

26. Some say that the horse became expendable with the advent of the modern car.
    C/CM   C/CM   NC/P

27. The Germanic languages have similar sentence patterns to English.
    C or NC/CM C/CM

28. He said history is his favorite subject.
    NC/P   C/CM

29. I said that "American History from 1865 to World War I" is my favorite course.
    NC/P C/CM   C/CM

30. "Ode to a Grecian Urn" is the name of a poem.

Answers to Exercise 4.2

Directions: Fill in correct form of the verb tense.

1. I had gone (go) to the store before I saw you yesterday. *Had* + v3 = past perfect (prior to simple past *saw*)

2. We will have completed (complete) the form by the end of the day. *Have* + v3 = future perfect

3. I will have seen (see) you by the time I leave. Future perfect

4. Had (had, have, has) you eaten before you came? *Had* + v3 = past perfect (prior to simple past *came*) (*came* = v2; *had eaten* = v3)

5. I saw you when you were coming (come) down the hill. Two actions are occurring simultaneously, both in past tense; therefore, one must be past progressive, and one must be simple past.

I saw you when you were coming.

X_____simple past + past progressive_____X.

6. Who told (tell) you that I was here? Both v2; no time precedes other.

7. Before I saw him, he had come (come) here. V3 before v2 (see *before*!)

8. If I had (know) known, I would have arrived earlier.

If + past perfect + present perfect (Remember: logically, past [*had*] is before present [*have*], but we can turn around the order in the sentence itself: *I would have arrived earlier if I had known* or *I would have arrived earlier had I known*.)

9. Can you (see) see if I move? *Can* is a modal verb; therefore, the first verb after it must be v1 (*see*).

10. If I were (walk) walking, I would not have my keys in my hand. The speaker is in the progressive act of leaving, so we must have -*ing*. We used *were*, because the speaker is not walking, so *walking* is contrary to fact, and the helping verb *were* must be used. See a similar example: If I *were* a child, I would be playing now. I am not a child, so I must use *were* and not *was*. *Was* is used if the condition is possible: If the mail *was* here at 10:00, I did not see it. It may have been there. I simply did not see it.

11. If I had (see) seen the dog, I would tell you.

12. As you run, I will be running (run) with you. Simple present to indicate future + future progressive.

13. As most people know (know), we will be (learn) learning more as time goes by.

14. She (walk) walked yesterday, but I had gone (go) before then.

15. If he is (go) going to the post office later, give (give) him this letter, please. Present progressive for the future + command form (always v1).

16. Because they had (break up) broken up their companies, the competitors got (get) most of the profits. Past perfect (v3) + simple past (v2)

17. What I (want) wanted to see was the success of all of the students.

18. Although I had not (see) seen him, I knew (know) then that he was in town.

19. Because they were (go) going so slowly, the meteor overtook (overtake) them in a matter of seconds. Past progressive + simple past.

20. After you had (give) given me the green light, I (send) sent your letter to the boss. Remember: Past perfect before simple past.

21. What bothers me is that as you are (get up) getting up, I will be (go) going to bed. Two actions are happening at exactly the same time for a duration in the future. *As* indicates duration.

22. Not knowing the truth is what had (give) given me the problem before you finally (tell) told me. Past perfect is prior to simple past.

23. I had lent (lend) him money far in advance. *In advance* suggests the simple past, and prior to that must be past perfect.

24. Too much responsibility always (cause) causes problems with irresponsible tenants. *Always* indicates repeated action; therefore, simple present is mandatory.

25. Since you will be (arrive) arriving early, could I (impose) impose on you for a ride? Future progressive to indicate simple future + modal +v1.

Answers to Exercise 4.3

Directions: Write *C* for *copula verb* or *A* for *action verb*. 1.3

1. He sounded the bell loudly due to the impending storm. A

2. He looked tired after being on the road for two days. C

3. As we walked through the pyramids, a rainbow appeared over the horizon. A

4. It seemed as if we were lost. C

5. He reacted calmly. A

6. We remained calm through the night. A/C

7. Something smelled fishy about his late-night meetings. C

8. He smelled badly, because his nose was broken. C

9. I felt bad about having her dog put outside. C

10. He appears to know what he is doing. C

11. The paper felt rough. C

12. He looked about the room furtively. A

13. He acted tough. A/C

14. He acted very obnoxiously at dinner. A

15. We wanted to ensure that the room did not smell bad. C

16. He was acting like a security guard. A/C

17. They remained in the ambulance. A

18. The excuse sounded like a lie. C

Answers to Exercise 4.4

Directions: Choose the appropriate answer.

1. The little boy is late. He _____get home before his mother becomes angry. (ought to, <u>had better</u>, can, must)

2. I really _____start exercising more, because I want to look good for my reunion. (must, <u>should</u>, could, would)

3. _____I actually register my car? (<u>must</u>, should, can, had better)

4. _____you let me borrow your pen? (should, <u>could</u>, may)

5. The boy said, "Do I _____wear this tie?" (need, must, <u>have to</u>, better)

6. You_____have the doctor check you over every year. (must, <u>should</u>, need, might)

7. Everyone _____eat a balanced diet, although most do not. (must, shall, might, <u>ought to</u>, may)

8. I_____go to the movie if I had enough money. (can, should, will, <u>would</u>)

9. _____a teacher allow the students to cheat on a test? (can, could, <u>should</u>, must)

10. The man thought he _____(could, <u>would</u>, will, can) have fame and glory if he _____(shall, will, would, <u>could</u>, might) only get to the top of the mountain.

Adjectives

Adjectives describe or modify nouns. These usually come before the noun, but not always.

The <u>happy</u> boy got a toy.

The <u>big</u> man said hello.

I am a <u>good</u> teacher.

I saw the <u>old</u> tree.

These are the easy adjectives, as most are. Notice that each adjective is placed before the noun it describes. However, we will see later that some adjectives are put off or delayed until after the nouns they describe. We are usually taught at a very young age that we can add a suffix to adjectives to compare that noun to something else.

The boy is **happier** than the man.

The **bigger** man said hello.

NOTE:

See appendices for comparatives and superlatives.

Note that there are irregular adjectives just as there are irregular verbs. We will discuss these in more detail in a later chapter. I mentioned that we delay some modifiers (adjectives). These are postposed adjectives (adjectives that are positioned after [post] the thing described).

I am loath to run a mile.

The adjective is *loath*, and it modifies the subject *I*. *Am* is the *be* verb.

In addition, we can use the perfect form of some verbs to function as a modifier. The word itself is not actually an adjective. However, it describes, or modifies, so we can say that it acts like an adjective. We call this an adjective. Look over the following sentences.

1. The <u>written</u> word is a powerful weapon.

2. The work is <u>completed</u>.

3. The boy is <u>tired</u>.

4. The <u>unexercised</u> muscle loses its strength.

5. The <u>boiling</u> water is very hot.

Explanation

1. *Written* is the adjective. By examining the word, we know that *write* is the verb, and *written* is the perfect form (third form).

2. *Complete* is the verb. This is a regular verb, which may or may not make it difficult to recognize the part of speech that it is in the sentence. However, if we look at the verb *is*, we know that *is* means present tense, and simple past and present tense may not go together at the same time. Therefore, *completed* must be an adjective in this sentence.

3. *Tired* is the adjective, with the same explanation as number 2. We know the word *tired* so well that we rarely think of the verb *tire*.

4. *Unexercised* is the adjective. *Exercise* is a noun and a verb. Here, we use it to describe the word *muscle*.

5. *Boiling* is the adjective. It describes *water*, which is a noun.

These words are known as participles. They are forms of words, such as *boiling*, that do not function in their normal capacity. *Boiling* is a *present participle* in the following sentence: <u>*Boiling*</u> lava from the volcano destroyed the town.

There is also the past participle: The <u>*traveled*</u> man has many experiences. These words in italics are usually verbs. In this context, they function as adjectives.

Many times, I give the example of myself. I am a father, but when I go to work, I take on a different role as a professor. The same is true with the English language. These words are verbs in other contexts, but they assume a different function in these particular sentences. When we start to look at a language in this way, we start to understand it. Then, we improve and become successful. These types of approaches are employed throughout the text. It only gets easier.

Verbs as Adjectives:

Past Participle

Regular verbs take -ed:

The <u>boiled</u> water was hot.

The <u>endangered</u> bull charged.

The <u>embittered</u> debate turned violent.

Irregular verbs take -en, -t, and some change in the middle to u:

The <u>broken</u> warrior was returned to his camp.

The <u>written</u> word is powerful.

The word <u>spoken</u> was like dynamite.

The promise <u>kept</u> is like money in the bank.

The <u>swept</u> floor looked very impressive.

The song <u>sung</u> is the best kind.

The <u>run</u> race is the best kind, too.

Present Participle

The <u>fighting</u> dogs were apprehended.

The leader was <u>astonishing</u>.

The <u>astounding</u> news caught me off guard.

NOTE: *These participles can be confusing if you have a simple construction of S–helping verb–MV (present participle). Ex: He is confusing; it is astonishing.*

Rule: If the participle has a noun before it and after it, the participle is really a verb.

Ex: He is <u>*confusing*</u> me. <u>*Me*</u> is therefore receiving the action of the verb *confusing*. In the first sentence, **He is confusing,** the subject <u>*he*</u> is being described as confusing, meaning that <u>*he*</u> causes others to be confused.

So, when you write a paper, double-check for objects (the nouns after the participles) to clarify yourself.

NOTE:
We will refer to a participle as such only if a verb is performing outside of its normal part of speech (i.e., if a verb is performing the duties of an adjective). A Concise Grammar of Contemporary English *calls this participation, and, from that idea, we get the name* participle.

Comparative and Superlative Adjectives

Adjectives describe a noun. Basically, as we view the comparative and superlative, we see that they are similar in their formation to adverbs of comparison. In addition, they use the phrase formation just the same: *She is more pretty than Sue*; or, *She is prettier than her sister.*

Comparative deals with two things, and superlative with three or more. There are two approaches to this: (1) to use the comparative and superlative suffixes on the end of the base form and (2) to use the words *more* and *most* + base form (i.e., *quick* = base form).

However, our adjective describes the noun, so we need to be concerned with the positioning of the adjective. In number 1, we are not concerned with the verb.

Two Major Positions

1. Attributive: This comes before the noun described.

The fat boy ate candy.

The boy ate good candy.

2. Postposed: This comes two places after the noun.
   a. After a linking verb: She is the best.
   b. Immediately after the word described: The word spoken is impossible to take back.

Comparative & Superlative Suffixes

Examples:

He is faster than Bob.

He is the fastest of the boys.

Note the pattern in the first sentence: N–V–adj–*than*–N

The pattern is usually: N–LV–adj + -*er*–than–N (comparative)
N / LV / (the) adj. +est. (superlative)

With the superlative we have several cues that indicate superlative. They are (1) the word *the* before the superlative phrase; (2) the use of present perfect after the superlative phrase; (3) the use of a prepositional phrase after the superlative phrase, generally employing the prepositions *of* and *in*; (4) three or more items.

Examples:

1. **Bob is the slowest.**
   Sally is the quickest.

2. **He is the fastest I have ever seen.**
   He was the fastest I have ever heard.

3. **He has been the slowest of the boys. (specific subset)**
   He will be the quickest in the entire class. (all-inclusive category)

4. **John is fast.**
   Rob is faster.
   But I am the fastest.

More & Most + Adjective

1. He had been more attentive than Bob.
   She seems more astute than her sister.
   He is the most superficial person.
   She looks the most beautiful.

2. He has been the most polite of all the boys I have seen.
   She will be the most adept of the girls I have seen.

3. He tends to be the most diligent of the boys.
   He is the most efficient in the whole class.

Adverbs

Adverbs mostly describe verbs, adverbs, and adjectives. There are many different functions of adverbs, but, for the present, we will look at these general categories.

Adverbs Modifying Verbs

I ran quickly.

The word *quickly* modifies the verb *ran*. *Quickly* is part of a class of adverbs termed *adverbs of manner*. It is necessary to have an action verb when employing an adverb of manner. Manner describes *how*; therefore, adverbs of manner tell how the action was/is or will be performed.

Examples:

I showered *slowly*.

I sang *loudly*.

I walked *briskly*.

NOTE:

It is very easy to recognize an adverb of manner, because they often are composed of an adjective + -ly. This is certainly not always true, but, for the beginner, any extra information will prove useful. In addition, we said that one must use an action verb (dynamic verb) in conjunction with an adverb of manner. There are generally exceptions to the rules, and we will examine some exceptions later.

Adverbs of Frequency

I walk *daily*.

He exercises *weekly*.

The man studies *nightly*.

I *usually* run in the morning.

I *seldom* drink coffee.

I *rarely* eat candy.

He *often* sleeps.

These answer the question, how often?

The words in italics are adverbs of frequency. They give information about how often an action is performed. The italicized words are formed by adding *-ly* to a noun. That is an effective way to spy many adverbs of frequency. The underlined words are not made in the same way, but they are still adverbs of frequency. Here again, we have an adverb that describes an action verb, hereinafter called a dynamic verb.

Adverbs of Degree Modifying Adverbs

He runs *very* well.

She speaks *extremely* quickly.

I work out *exceedingly* hard.

He teaches *highly* effectively.

Pay attention to the construction of the sentences. The pattern in all of these sentences is S–V–Adv–Adv. The first word is the subject, followed by verb, adverb, and finally adverb. The first adverb describes the adverb at the end of the sentence, and the last adverb modifies the verb. This is not always the case, but, once again, we want to learn to recognize the basic patterns in a sentence so, when we begin to compose essays, the patterns will be there. Finally, we may say that adverbs that modify other adverbs answer either the question, to what degree? or the question, how much?

Adverbs of Degree Describing Adjectives

With this construction, we use a *be* verb (stative verb) or a copula verb.

I am *slightly* tired.

He is *excessively* obnoxious.

The woman is *so* attractive.

The waiter only seemed *unusually* bitter (he is usually that rude).

The house appeared *surprisingly* clean.

In these sentences, the pattern is S–V–Adv–Adj. The subject does the action (of the verb); the adverb modifies the adjective, and the adjective describes the subject. Again, the adverb answers the question, to what degree?

Forming Adverbs

Now, let's look at three main types of adverbs and how they are formed.

Adverbs of Frequency

These tell how often something occurs. <u>Class I</u>: It is common to form these by adding *-ly* to a noun (e.g., *hourly, daily, weekly, monthly, yearly*). <u>Class II</u>: Some are formed by adding *-ly* to an adjective, such as *rarely, usually, commonly, normally, mostly, frequently, constantly,* and *generally*. Some, however, do not take any suffix, such as *seldom, often, never,* and *always*.

These answer the question, how often?

<u>Syntactic Positioning</u>

For the first class, and we are generalizing, place the adverb in the initial position, at the beginning of the sentence, offset by a comma, or at the final position, at the end of the sentence.

Weekly, I go to the grocery store.

I go to the barber monthly.

For class II, place the adverb in the initial position, before the main verb phrase, or, if there is an additional nominal time tag suggesting duration, after the main verb phrase and before the time tag.

Usually, I eat at 5:00.

Generally, I swim in the morning.

I normally eat at 5:00.

I eat constantly at night.

I eat frequently in the summer.

GRAMMAR NOTE: *It is possible to put the adverb of frequency in the final position, as well, especially if the tag (adverbial) is one of location.*

I eat at Taco Bell mostly.

I run at the track generally.

These adverbs, which come after the verb phrase and appear in the final position, are better limited to those ending in *-ly*. Keep in mind that we are speaking in generalities, and there are many exceptions. But because the scope of grammar here is limited to formal writing, we are unable to delve too deeply into all of the exceptions.

Adverbs of Manner

These describe an action verb and are usually formed by adding *-ly* to an adjective. They must modify (describe) an action verb. Some examples include the following: *quickly, slowly, bitterly, rapidly, resentfully, happily, easily, tiredly, eerily, knowingly,* and *cautiously.* These answer the question, how? or the question, to what degree?

He reluctantly walked home.

He drove slowly.

He answered resentfully.

He ran sluggishly.

He quietly answered.

He resentfully buried his friend.

He answered happily.

The same rules apply here as for the positioning of the adverbs of frequency, except it is wise to avoid the initial positioning, because the adverbs of manner could be confused with a certain class of adverbials, possibly leading to logical problems.

Irregular Adverbs

Do not add *-ly* to *fast, hard* (if it comes after the verb phrase), and *well. Fast* is an adjective and an adverb; therefore, we never add an *-ly. Well* is an adverb that describes action verbs, with the exception of the copula *feel,* which is not always a copula, but *well* is used in conjunction with *feel* when describing health. *Hard* is used two ways as an adverb. First, when used after the verb phrase, it means *much* in amount, or it is used to comment on the degree, connoting a worthwhile attempt at doing something well. **He ran hard.** This means that he tried his best. Secondly, when the word *hard* is used as an adverb and placed before the verb phrase, it must be used with an *-ly.* Here, it takes on an opposite meaning than the one previously mentioned. **He hardly ran.** This indicates that he ran a little and walked a lot, putting forth very little effort. Incidentally, *hard* is also an adjective.

After the verbs below, use adjectives, with the exceptions noted. These verbs are copula verbs, which means they fall into the same category as linking verbs, taking a subject complement that describes and/or renames the subject. We know a noun or an adjective, which may apply here, too, realizes the SC.

Copulas: Seem, Appear, Taste, Smell, Feel, and Look

Exceptions: *Appear, taste, feel,* and *look.*

It seemed pleasant until the rains came.

She appeared nice. (She was nice [i.e., polite] to us.)

The steak tasted good.

The perfume smelled sweet.

He felt well. (His condition was good.)

She looked pretty.

The exceptions—*appear, taste, look,* and *feel*—can be thought out by analyzing the subject of the sentence. These are exceptions in which we will use adverbs with *-ly*, which means the verbs as used in these sentences are not functioning as copula verbs (i.e., linking verbs) any longer, but they are functioning as **lexical** verbs, or action verbs.

The woman appeared suddenly.

This means that she came into our view very quickly. If I say she **appeared** nice, that suggests she was nice, and I think she may be a nice person, but I am not certain. Understand that if the subject is a noun that cannot do anything, we usually need an adjective. For example, the dinner appeared nice. It cannot appear suddenly, because the dinner can do nothing; it is only food.

The same logic is true for *look. She looked nice* means she was pretty. If someone loses her child, I can say she looked frantically. That indicates how, in what method, she searched for her child. Again, we can analyze the subject of the sentence, and this may tell us the meaning.

The dress looked great. A dress does not have eyes, so we know that we must use an adjective after the verb, and it is a copula verb in this structure. The grammaticality of a structure often depends on the environment of the diction.

The steak tasted good.

Steak has no mouth, so we need an adjective. Compare that to the next sentence. He tasted the hot food slowly. The man is capable of eating the food in a certain manner, so the verb in this context is a lexical one.

In addition to scrutinizing the subject, we can also see if there is a DO. Copulas do not take DOs, because they are not dynamic, action verbs. He felt the material carefully. *The material* is the DO. What if we say, *He felt around carefully*? Evidently, he is searching for something. Therefore, *around* is an adverbial describing where he felt.

Comparative and Superlative Adverbs
These take only action verbs.

Comparative deals with two things, and superlative with three or more. There are two approaches to this: (1) to use the comparative and superlative suffixes on the end of the adjectival form and (2) to use the words *more* and *most* + adverb.

Comparative & Superlative Suffixes
Ex(s):

He runs faster than Bob.

He runs the fastest of the boys.

Note the pattern in the first sentence: S–V–Adv–*than*–N

The pattern is usually: N–Action Verb–Adv + *-er*–*than*–N (comparative)

S–Action Verb–(*the*) _____ + *est* (superlative)

Several cues indicate a superlative: (1) the word *the* before the superlative phrase; (2) the use of present perfect after the superlative phrase; (3) the use of a prepositional phrase after the superlative phrase, generally employing the prepositions *of* and *in*.

Examples:

1. He types the slowest.

   He answers the quickest.

2. He runs the fastest I have ever seen.

   He talks the fastest I have ever heard.

3. He types the slowest of the boys. (specific subset)

   He answers the quickest in the entire class. (all-inclusive category)

More & Most + Adverb

He types more slowly than Bob.

She answers more astutely than her sister.

He types the most slowly.

She answers the most astutely.

He runs the most slowly of all the boys I have seen.

She answers the most adeptly of the girls I have seen.

He works the most diligently of the boys.

He works the most efficiently in the whole class.

NOTE:

It is permitted to say, She works more diligently than the other girls in the class. *This is correct, because we have separated the entire class into three groups: her, the other girls, and the remainder of the class (presumably boys); therefore, she is not the best. The comparison is, however, only between her and the other girls.*

EXERCISE 4.5

Exercise 4.5

Directions: Choose the appropriate answer.

1. He runs_____(as fast, faster, the fastest) than I do.

2. Bob runs more_____(quick, quicker, quicklier, quickly) than I do.

3. She is_____(pretty, the most prettiest, prettiest, the prettiest) of all the candidates.

4. Of all of the days, this is the_____(worse, worst, most worst, worsed).

5. Jan reads_____(slow, slower, slowly, more slowly).

6. It is more_____(unlikelier, unlike, unlikely) than not that you will get a good grade.

7. The race was close, but, of the three, Bill was_____(the better, the best, the most good).

8. I loathe sloth_____(more than, most than, the most than) any other thing.

9. The exercises seemed_____(fast, the slowest, quickest, faster) than the ones we did yesterday.

10. If I had known you_____(long, longest, longer), I would have allowed you to come along with us.

11. He appeared more_____(quick, quicker, quickly), because he came by jet.

12. I felt around_____(blind, blindly, more careless, careless) in the dark.

13. The fighter looked_____(sluggish, sluggishly, sluggishlier) due to his gaining weight.

14. I feel_____(good, well, worse, goodly) now that I am healed.

15. He_____(hard, almost, hardly, little) felt anything, because he had taken painkillers.

16. The punch landed _____(well, hard, good, badly) enough to hurt.

17. The boat inched along at a_____(remarkable, remarkably, remarkingly, remarking) slow pace.

18. Of all the people I know, my wife is_____(lovelier, the lovelier, the loveliest, the most lovelier).

19. This machine is the_____(fastest, faster, most fast) of the two.

20. The milk tasted_____(sourly, sour, more sourer).

21. As we ran, I saw the_____(most beautifullest, more beautiful, more beautiful, most beautiful) sunset I had ever seen.

22. The three mountains were spectacular, but I think that Pinnacle was the_____(awesomest, most awesome, more awesome).

23. The chef tasted_____(more quicker, the quicker, quicklier, more quickly) than the amateur.

24. The tint seemed_____(more radiant, more radiantly, radianter) compared to that of yesterday.

25. The army looked_____(forcefully, forceful, forcefuller) in their gear.

Articles: A, An, The

These are sometimes called *determiners*. They point out a noun or a word that functions as a noun. There are general rules that must be followed, although there are exceptions when using articles. The word *a* must precede a word with a consonant. This is true in writing and speaking.

I want a spoon.

I saw a man.

The word an must precede a word that begins with a vowel.

I ate an apple.

I went to an orchard.

Exception: When we use a word that starts with an *h* that is not aspirated, or almost breathless, such as *holistic, hour,* or *herb,* we need to use the article *an.*

The is used with a word beginning with a vowel or consonant.

I went to the hotel.

The hour has come.

The apple was good.

The battery is weak.

There are certain idiomatic expressions that do not necessitate the use of an article. Some examples:

I went home.

I went to school.

He attends church every week.

However, when the word is used as a subject specifically giving information about possession or location, we will be more likely to use the article.

The home of Mr. Smith is nice.

The school on the corner is huge.

The Church of Latter-Day Saints is across the street.

Prepositions

Prepositions tell us the positions of things. Usually, at least in a statement, the preposition will come before a noun. The prefix *pre* means *before*, and *position* indicates *place*. Therefore, prepositions give us information on the place of a certain noun. This is a good example that I learned as a student. Most of the words that will fit into this blank are prepositions.

The bird flew_____the cloud.

The words that fit in here indicate the position of the bird in relation to the noun *cloud*. These are some possibilities: *under, underneath, over, in, at, near, around, in back of, nearby, atop, on top of, behind, in front of, through, out, out of.*

There are others, but they might be awkward in this particular sentence. Certain prepositions need to be phrasal, or need other prepositions with them to sound grammatical. Some examples that are inappropriate here are *during, while,* and *of* (about-arguable-informal & regional).

Answers to Exercise 4.5

1. He runs_____(as fast, **faster,** the fastest) than I do. Comparison of two. Remember, *fast* is an adverb and an adjective, so it does not take -*ly* in American English.

2. Bob runs more_____(quick, quicker, quicklier, **quickly**) than I do. We used the adverbial form here with the -*ly*, because *run* is an action verb.

3. She is _____(pretty, most prettiest, prettiest, **the prettiest**) of all the candidates. *The prettiest* is the best answer, because it has the definite article *the*; therefore, it is the formal answer in the superlative form.

4. Of all of the days, this is the_____(worse, **worst,** most worst, worsed).

5. Jan reads_____(slow, slower, **slowly,** more slowly). *Read* is an action verb, so we need the adverb of degree—*slowly*. *Slow* is an adjective. We cannot use *more*, because there is no comparison to a second person.

6. It is more_____(likelier, alike, **likely**) than not that you will get a good grade. *Likely* is the adjective that will fill the position of subject complement here. To use *alike*, we need a subject with at least two things (e.g., *The teams are alike*).

7. The race was close, but, of the three, Bill was_____(the better, **the best,** the most good). *Best* is the only superlative form, which is required with three things.

8. I loathe sloth _____(**more than,** most than, the most than) any other thing. *More than* is acting like the superlative, but, unlike the construction of number 7, the construction of this sentence has only two compared components: (1) *sloth* and (2) *any other thing.* Consequently, because only two things are specifically stated, we need to use the form that is grammatically comparative, even though the suggestion is superlative. Note that *thing* is singular.

9. The exercises seemed to go _____(fast, the slowest, quickest, **faster**) than the ones we did yesterday. Only two days are compared.

10. If I had known you_____(long, longest, **longer**), I would have allowed you to come along with us.

11. He appeared more_____(quick, quicker, **quickly**), because he came by jet. *Appeared* is an action verb here and not a copula. We know this, because he came by jet.

12. I felt around_____(blind, **blindly,** more careless, careless) in the dark. *Felt* here means to feel with the hands. This is action.

13. The fighter looked_____(**sluggish,** sluggishly, sluggishlier) due to his gaining weight. The fighter's body was overweight.

14. I feel _____(good, **well,** worse, goodly) now that I am healed. Health indicates wellness. This is formal.

15. He _____(hard, almost, **hardly,** little) felt anything, because he had taken painkillers. Be careful of the double negative in this construction. *Hardly* means *little in amount.* Some people say, "I did not hardly." That means you did a lot, then, which is the opposite of what you want to say.

16. The punch landed _____(**well,** hard, good, badly) enough to hurt. The punch hurt; therefore, it must have landed well. How? Well. (manner)

17. The boat inched along at a_____(remarkable, **remarkably,** remarkingly, remarking) slow pace. This answer is an adverb of degree. How slow was it? Remarkably!

18. Of all the people I know, my wife is_____(lovelier, the lovelier, **the loveliest,** the most lovelier). Compare to number 8 above. Very simple. There are two divisions: my wife and all of the others. Although there are only two groups, the other group has the plural *people,* so were need the superlative.

19. This machine is the_____(fastest, **faster,** most fast) of the two. Look! Only two!

20. The milk tasted_____(sourly, **sour,** more sourer). *Tasted* means it was.

21. As we ran, I saw the _____(most beautifullest, more beautiful, more beautiful, **most beautiful**) sunset I have ever seen. The present perfect [*that*] *I have ever seen* with the *that* elided indicates superlative; it means *ever, of all times.* Again, I need to mention number 18.

22. The three mountains were spectacular, but I think that Pinnacle was the_____(awesomest, **the most awesome,** more awesome). Three or more takes superlative. Remember the following rule: if the word has seven letters or more, don't add a suffix; use *more* or *most.*

23. The chef tasted_____(more quicker, the quicker, quicklier, **more quickly**) than the amateur. It was a contest, at least an action verb.

24. The tint seemed_____(**more radiant,** more radiantly, radianter) compared to that of yesterday.

25. The army looked_____(forcefully, **forceful,** forcefuller) in their gear. Copula verb.

Pronouns

Pronouns are words that take the place of a noun in a sentence. The prefix *pro* means *for* or *in the place of.* There are subject pronouns and object pronouns. In an active statement, the subject comes before the verb, and the object comes after the verb, or the object pronoun comes after the preposition.

Personal Pronouns:

Subject Singular	Object Singular
I, you, he, she, it	me, you, him, her, it
Plural	**Plural**
We, you, them	us, you, them

Reflexive Pronouns

S = singular, P = plural

I = myself (S)

You = yourself (S)

You = yourselves (P)

Us = ourselves (P)

Them = themselves (P)

Him = himself (S)

These can function as stress markers that come immediately after the subject or at the end of the sentence/clause (use a reflexive pronoun immediately after the subject to avoid problems with description).

They can also be the DOs of a sentence.

Stress Markers

I *myself* want to vote x in this election (myself).

You *yourself* should know the answer to that question (yourself).

You *yourselves* know that all the work must be accurate.

We *ourselves* understood everything (ourselves), unlike the rest.

They *themselves* took the cat out (themselves), instead of having the maid do it.

He *himself* took the watch (himself), not his brother like you thought.

 **NOTE:**

These rename the subjects, not the objects above.

As Objects

I know *myself*. (As DO)

You see *yourself* in the mirror. (As DO)

You must ask *yourselves* the question. (As indirect object [IO])

They lost *themselves* in the pleasure of Rome. (As DO)

He hit *himself* in the eye. (As DO)

I am proud *of myself*. (As object of preposition)

We laughed at *ourselves*. (As obj. of prep.)

They thought of *only themselves*. (As obj. of prep.)

Functions:
1. To show emphasis, therefore placed immediately after the word it renames, functioning as a restrictive appositive, or uncommonly placed in a postposed position.
2. DO, comes after an action (dynamic) verb

3. To show emphasis, placed after the IC, not as emphatic as number 1. Examples:

I myself know the truth.

I hit myself.

You yourself told me that.

You hurt yourself by playing.

He himself pulled the trigger.

He hurt himself.

She herself called off the wedding

She called herself on the phone.

The dog itself saved the little boy.

The dog bit itself.

We ourselves must solve this problem.

We cheated ourselves.

You yourselves can change this school.

You hurt yourselves by not conforming to the rules.

They themselves cleaned the house.

They answered themselves.

Postposed

I did it myself.

You won the game yourself.

He came here himself.

The dog killed the snake itself.

We remedied the problems ourselves.

You did the work yourselves.

They repaired the car themselves.

A postposed reflexive pronoun means the same as if it came directly behind the noun it renamed, but the emphasis is not as strong with post-position. If we add the preposition *by* in front of the postposed reflexive pronoun, the meaning changes to *alone*.

Ex: I did it by myself. = I did it alone.

He came here by himself. = He came here alone.

Demonstrative Pronouns

This, that, these, those

These are pronouns; therefore, they can act as subjects and objects in a sentence. However, when used before a noun, they become demonstrative adjectives. The word *demonstrative* is simply the adjectival form of the word *demonstrate*, which means *to show*.

This is my coat. (near)

That is the building. (far)

These are the cards. (near)

Those are my friends. (far)

This coat is mine.

That house is mine.

These cards are for you.

Those boys are my friends.

Possessive Pronouns

(1) Before the subject; (2) before the object = *my, your, his, her, their, our, its*; and (3) only after a linking verb (LV; a *be* verb) = *mine, hers, theirs, ours*

Syntactic Positioning:

1. Before the subject

2. Before the object

The possessive pronouns in classes 1 and 2 must have a noun after them, except for *his* and *its*.

3. The possessive pronouns in this class must come after an LV. We

designate a *be* verb as an LV when it is the only verb in the verb phrase of the main clause of the superstructure. See below.

> This *is* mine. *Is* = LV. (only verb in the verb phrase)
>
> This key, the one you say was found, *is* mine. *Is* = LV

In the interjectory clause, *the one you say was found*, the verb phrase is *was found*. *Was* is not an LV, because it is an auxiliary verb, called a helping verb, and *found* is the main verb of the verb phrase of that DC.

> My book is here.
>
> He gave me my book.
>
> It is mine.
>
> Your book is here.
>
> I have your book.
>
> This is yours. (singular and plural)
>
> His dog ran away.
>
> I saw his dog.
>
> The dog is his.
>
> Her cat is over there.
>
> I saw her cat.
>
> The cat is hers.
>
> Its tire is going flat.
>
> The dog wagged its tail.
>
> This is its bone.
>
> Our day is very long.
>
> This is our day.
>
> This table is ours.
>
> This class is yours. (Can be plural or singular, only postposed)
>
> The table is theirs. (Only plural, only postposed)

Indefinite Pronouns

Somebody, someone, anyone, anybody, nobody, no one, everyone

Note: These are all singular.

Usually, when asking questions and stating negative answers, use the *any-* words.

Ex: I don't want *anyone* to help me.

I do not ask for *anyone/anybody* to help me.

Don't you want anyone/anybody/someone/somebody to help?
(No idea of reply)

Don't you think anyone/anybody/someone/somebody will see you?
(No idea of reply)

Does everyone understand? (Genuine question)

Does everyone know where it is? (Genuine question)

However, the *some-* words may be used with negative answers (and some positive questions) in order to stress an alternative.

Ex: I do not want somebody. I want you to help me.

Will somebody please help me? (Get up now!)

Do you think someone/anyone came by?

Does someone leave money in the box? (suspects one particular person)

Does anyone leave food for the needy? (Many people are expected to contribute)

Interjections

Interjections serve no grammatical function except to interrupt. For example, the word *oh* is an interjection in the following sentence: *I am, oh, a man.*

Conjunctions

Conjunctions link words, phrases, ideas, and even clauses. Some examples are *and, but, so, yet,* and *or.*

I eat and drink.

I ate, but I am hungry.

I exercise, so I will be healthy.

I may see him, yet he may not see me.

I want to see you now, or I want to see you tomorrow.

Conjunctions go hand in hand with punctuation. In addition, there are subordinating, correlative, and coordinating conjunctions. Grammar is so highly significant to effective writing that I have elected to include the bulk of conjunctions in the grammar section of the text as well as in the section on writing. Hence, we will move into the section on writing, and, if questions arise on punctuation, refer to the section on grammar.

Coordinating Conjunctions

BOYFANS = *but, because, or, yet, for, and, neither, nor, so*

These link ICs as well as phrases. Therefore, a comma must precede the c/c that begins the second IC.

He arrived, <u>but</u> he was late.

He was late, <u>because</u> the plane was delayed.

I will eat turkey here, <u>or</u> I'll go out for dinner.

She was tired, <u>yet</u> she was a very gracious host.

I was four hours late, <u>for</u> the storm had derailed a train. (archaic)

She went shopping all day, <u>and</u> she picked up the dinner at the store.

She does not want meat, <u>neither</u> does he. (inverted V-S)

You do not like pretense, <u>nor</u> do I. (inverted V-S)

I ate too fast, <u>so</u> I will wait to exercise. She likes him, so do I. (inverted V-S)

Subordinating Conjunctions

Subordinating conjunctions make an IC dependent. An IC has a subject and a verb (almost always). They are usually time words of duration: *once, after, when, until, before, so* (*that*), *because, although, though, in* (*that*), *even* (*though*).

GRAMMAR NOTE:

These may change functions, and most of them do as we move them in a sentence.

<u>Once</u> I became a man, I started to act responsibly.

<u>After</u> I received the medal, I went home.

<u>When</u> I was a kid, I got good grades.

<u>Until</u> you move, there is nothing I can do.

<u>Before</u> I was married, I was lonely.

<u>So that</u> you can sleep well, I will leave early.

<u>Because</u> you hit me, I am very angry.

<u>Although</u> I am happy, I could do better.

<u>Though</u> he is my best friend, he makes me upset.

<u>In that</u> he is a good guy, we will help him.

<u>Even though</u> you like him, I do not trust him.

We can turn these sentences around and usually retain the same meaning. Also, most of them do not require a comma when the subordinate clause (DC) is inside the superstructure (the complete sentence).

I started to act responsibly, once I became a man. (comma optional)

I went home after I received the medal.

I got good grades when I was a kid.

There is nothing I can do until you move.

I was lonely before I was married.

I will leave early so that you can sleep well.

I am very angry, because you hit me. (must have the comma)

I could do better although I am happy.

He makes me upset though he is my best friend. (*although* is better here)

We will help him in that he is a good guy.

I do not trust him even though you like him.

Simple Conjunctions

Conjunctions can link one-word phrases, multiword phrases, and clauses. The one-word phrase linkers will simply be termed coordinators or simple conjunctions in this text. Below they link phrases that seem equivalent in weight in the sentences.

I walk and run.

I drink coffee but not tea.

I do not stare and do not whine.

I can eat and drink at 5:00.

Correlative Conjunctions

Either/Or

Either you go, or I will.

Either you or he will go.

Neither/Nor

Neither you nor he will eat dinner. (No one will)

Neither rain nor snow stops the postman. (Nothing stops)

Not only/but also (In addition to)

I *not only* begged *but also* pleaded with her.

The camel can *not only* keep on going *but also* make it there on time.

Attention: For more on clauses, types and punctuation thereof, see the units on punctuation and embedding.

CHAPTER FIVE:

Syntax and Grammar

Grammatical vs. Syntactic Functions of a Word

The hardest thing for most native speakers to grasp when learning English is that a word possibly changes functions as we move it in a sentence. As a practical analogy, I'll use myself. At home, I am a father and a husband. When I go to work, I am a professor. Now, my role as a father does not change. I am still a father and a husband, but that duty is temporarily suspended. I am simply moving, laterally speaking, into a different role. The same is true as we move certain words around in a sentence. Therefore, many times, when I refer to a part of speech as an adjective, for example, it may be a verb acting like an adjective in that particular slot in the sentence. Before we continue, let's look at some definitions.

Grammar: A set of rules that sets forth the correct standard of usage in a language. Roughly speaking, these rules determine how we say things in language correctly. This includes agreement between words in relation to other constructions in a sentence.

Syntax: The study of sentences and their structure, and the constructions within sentences. Roughly speaking, this tells us what goes where in a sentence.

<u>Active Sentence:</u> Sometimes called active voice, a sentence where the subject does the action. Ex: I ate (S–V). The subject did something (usually on a DO).

<u>Passive Sentence:</u> Sometimes called passive voice, a sentence where the subject receives the action. The apple was eaten (S–helping verb–main verb). Something was done to the subject. The passive never takes a DO.

Usually, the subject in a sentence is a noun. Analyze the next two sentences.

The old people counted their money.
Art.–adj.–S–V–pro.–DO

Art. = article
Adj. = adjective

S = subject
V = verb

Pro. = pronoun
DO = direct object
The old counted their money.
Art.–S–V–pro.–DO

Although *old* is not a noun, it is the subject in this sentence. Why? Because the word *old* moved in the sentence. We omitted the word *people*, so *old* took the position of subject. *Old* is still an adjective, just as I am still a father during the time at work, but my function changes, because my environment changes. The word *old* is therefore acting as a noun, so it can function as the subject of the sentence.

Even though you do not know that you know, you have just learned the difference between the syntactical function and the grammatical function of a word. So, when we mention the syntactical function of a word, we talk about how it operates in a sentence (syntactical is the adjectival form of the noun *syntax*). Let's take a look at another one for nouns.

I see the good, the bad, and the ugly.

S–V–DO–DO–DO

DO = Direct object. In an active sentence, if the subject does something to something else or someone, the thing or person receiving that action is the DO. The verb must be active, however (not a *be* verb). In this sentence, the action verb is *see*, so we must ask what is seen. The answer is *the good, the bad, and the ugly.* These words are adjectives like the word *old.* However, they are acting like nouns in this sentence, so they are the DOs.

Look again at this sentence: The old counted their money.

The word *money* is a noun, and it is the DO of the sentence. Its grammatical function is noun, and its syntactic function is DO. The structure is the same as in the sentence we just looked at, except the words *the good, the bad, and the ugly* function as the DOs even though they are all adjectives. They do this by acting like nouns in accordance with where they are located in the sentence.

It takes a little while to begin to recognize the similarity of certain grammatical and syntactical structures in sentences. You can do it. If you have problems, stop. Try to find the subject and the verb; after you do that, you have won half of the battle. Most importantly, take your time. You are not in a race. Relax.

Components of Sentences

Phrases: A phrase is one or more words with a specific duty in a sentence. The noun in the following sentence is a noun phrase.

The <u>dog</u> ate.

The phrase can be a group of words with one specific duty. The following verbs constitute a verb phrase.

I <u>had been walking</u> for quite some time.

These words, all of them, act as one unit in the sentence, called a syntactic unit. *Had been walking* is, of course, three words, but they must work together to fulfill the duty of telling a specific time. It is common for different parts of speech to work together as one unit to fulfill a specific duty or function in the sentence. In that case, one word is the leader, called the headword, and it determines the duty of the whole unit, much like a squad leader in the army.

The big, fat, stupid *camel* walked across the road.

(*The*) *big, fat,* and *stupid* are adjectives. (An article, called a determiner, is considered a subcategory of adjective, or an adjectival.)

However, *camel* is a noun. Because all of the adjectives describe the noun, the entire phrase is a noun phrase, with the noun as the headword, the leader of the group. The duty, or the syntactic function, of the unit is to be the subject of the sentence. Let's make a further distinction.

1. *Camel* is the simple subject of the sentence.

2. *The, big, fat, stupid camel* is the complete subject of the sentence, called complete because the adjectives complete the entire thought concerning the headword.

The same logic holds true with other syntactic units. Look at the DO in this sentence.

I passed the <u>huge, pretty, old *truck*</u>.

Huge, pretty, and *old* are adjectives. However, *truck* is a noun; therefore, this is a noun phrase, and the syntactic unit is the DO of the sentence. But *huge, pretty, old* is an adjective phrase.

NOTE:	*A pretty huge truck* means *a very big truck*.

We need to approach the grammar exactly like we did the pods for our papers. Think of your sentence in geographical terms. Your subject and verb are always the starting point. Everything from there should include looking at what comes to the left of the subject and what comes to the right of the verb. The subject and the verb are the basic units of construction of every sentence in English. When we have a clause without a verb, we speak of it in terms of a verbless clause.

Clauses

As we said before, **there are two main types of clauses: (1) independent**, consisting of a subject and a verb and able to stand alone as a grammatical entity; **(2) dependent**, usually consisting of a subject and a verb and unable to stand alone as a grammatical entity. A DC depends on an IC to make sense; therefore it is called a dependent or subordinate clause. A subordinate clause usually has a subordinator at the beginning of it, thereby making an otherwise independent clause dependent.

I was a boy = IC

<u>When</u> I was a boy = DC

(Sub.)
There are several basic constituents of sentences. These constituents are units sometimes made of the phrases and clauses seen above.
1. Subject
2. Verb
3. Objects: Direct and Indirect
4. Complements: Subject and Object

I hit the ball.
S–V–DO

A DO only comes after an action verb, called a dynamic verb. The action is transferred from the subject to the DO: in other words, the subject does the action (of the action verb) to the DO.

I kicked the door.
S–V–DO

I ate the bread.
S–V–DO.

Indirect Object

I gave him the test.
S–V–IO–DO

I wrote her a letter.
S–V–IO–DO

Or

I gave the test to him.
S–V–DO–IO

I wrote a letter to her.
S–V–DO–IO

Rule: The thing the action is performed on or done to is the DO.

If I can put a preposition in front of the noun at the end, that noun is most likely the IO, but we call it the object of the preposition, even though the function is similar.

However, the IO can take a preposition in front of it only when the IO is at the end of the sentence. Compare the IOs in the sentences to those at the end of the sentences.

Tip: Think logically. We said that the DO receives the action of the sentence. Some people get confused. Look at this sentence.

I gave the man a letter. I gave a letter to the man.

What did I give? A letter. To whom? To the man.

Logically, the letter received the action of giving. The letter was what was given, not the man. I didn't pick up the man and give him away. I picked up the letter and gave it away. Therefore, the letter receives the action from the verb. I did the action (performed the action) on the letter and did it to the letter. The man receives the thing itself, the noun (the letter), not the action from the verb. The man receives the gift, not the giving.

4. **Complements:** Rename and/or describe the unit.

(A) <u>Subject Complement</u> (SC)

She is pretty.
S–V–Subj. comp. (Realized by an adjective)

He is a student.
S–V–Subj. comp. (Realized by a noun)

(B) <u>Object Complement</u> (OC)

I made my wife happy. (Realized by an adj.)
S–V–DO–Obj. comp.

They chose my boss the manager. (Realized by a noun)
S–V–DO–Obj. comp.

A noun or an adjective realizes or forms a complement (other ways seen later).

A subject complement usually comes after a linking verb.

Other Syntactic Constituents

Adverbials

Adverbials are a huge class of phrases and clauses realized by a number of grammatical constructions. Basically, they answer the questions of where, when, why, and how. Because this is basically a writing text, we will briefly look at some of these functions in regard to the effect on our writing.

(A) <u>Conjunctive Adverbs</u>: Connect clauses and ideas (usually), like conjunctions, and are common as transitions, and are usually set off by commas.

Therefore, he left.

Then, they ate dinner.

Consequently, they got away with murder.

Next, plus, in addition, as a result, and *moreover* are all conjunctive adverbs.
Function = Connect
(B) <u>Commentaries</u>: Usually are set apart by commas, and comment on the clause itself.

Honestly stated, I think I'll pass.

Bluntly put, I think he's a fraud.

No pun intended, she is X.

Jokingly put . . .

Simply stated . . .

Other Grammatical Constructions

Prepositional Phrases

A prepositional phrase (PP) consists of a preposition plus a noun.

I eat <u>at the table</u>.

He lives <u>under the bridge</u>.

<u>Around the corner</u>, there is a store.

<u>After the fight</u>, they were friends.

They went <u>over the hill, by the well</u>, and on to grandmother's house.

Gerunds and Infinitives

(A) Gerunds: Gerunds are verb + *ing*
   Functions:
   1. Subject: Running is a good exercise.
   2. Object: I like running.
   3. To express purpose: I go to the track for running.

With the gerund of purpose, it's common to use the prepositions for *and* about *before the gerund.*

(B) Infinitives: *To* + verb functions:

1. Subject: To exercise is healthy.

2. Object: I love to exercise.

3. To express purpose: I am here to run.

With the infinitive of purpose, it is common to use the preposition to *before the (bare) infinitive (VI).*

<u>Gerund as Complement:</u>

This is useless for learning.

That is essential for listening.

She was wonderful for counseling.

Construction: S + LV + SC + ([p + obj.])
PP = second comp.
Remember: The gerund is acting like a noun or an adverb in order to function in these positions.

<u>Infinitive as Complement:</u>

The game is impossible to win.

The boy is useless to hire.

The dog is too stupid to teach.

Construction: S + LV + SC + Infinitive comp.

Relative Clauses: Relative Pronoun + Verb

A relative pronoun (RP) renames a noun from the main clause, the IC. The relative pronouns include *who, whoever, whom, whomever, that, which, whichever, what, whatever,* and *whose.*

Who, whom, and *that* are used to rename people
Which, what, whatever, and *that* are used for things.
Whose shows personal possession.

S–V–SC
The man who you hit was my friend. (RP renames the S.)
RP–S–V

Who is subjective case in formal writing.
Whom is objective case.

S–V–DO
The man, whoever he was, took my pen. (RP renames the S.)
RP–S–V

S–V–DO
I hit the bad guy, whomever he was. (RP renames the DO.)
RP–S–V

S–V–SC
The boy that came was my son. (RP renames the S.)
RP–V

S–V–DO
He took the one which was mine. (RP renames the DO)
RP–V–SC

S–V–DO
He knew whose it was (possessive)
RP–S–V

S–V–prep. + N = PP

The girl whose mother died was at our house.

RP–S–V

S–V–DO

I know /whatever hurt her/ will stop.

RP–V–DO–Aux.–MV

(Complete subject)–Aux.–Main verb

Passive Voice

The passive voice, as we have said before, involves a construction where the subject is acted on, as opposed to performing the action as in an active sentence. We will touch on this briefly, because academic writing, specifically writing argument, involves active style. But, the passive voice causes many problems with punctuation and grammar. It is also used in some reports. Let's change this next sentence to passive.

Steps: Changing an Active Sentence to a Passive Sentence (no DO):

1. Change DO to S.
2. Bring down MV (main verb) and change to v3 (perfect tense)
3. Add auxiliary verb.
4. Add *by* phrase: The subject of the active sentence becomes the object of the preposition in the passive sentence.

S–V–DO

I ate some rice.

1. Some rice
2. Some rice_____eaten
3. Some rice was eaten by me.

1 3 2 4

Steps: Some rice/ was/ eaten/ by me.

Tip: There is always an auxiliary verb.

Active: I am gathering carrots.

Passive: Carrots are being gathered by me.

I was teaching the classes.

Change DO to S.

The class

Bring down main verb–change to v3

The class_____ _____taught

Add auxiliary verb. If there is already an auxiliary verb, we bring it down, too, before we add a new one.

Aux./ add/ v3(perfect form)

The classes were *being* (added) taught.

Because the main verb was progressive, the auxiliary verb we added must be progressive, as well. Also, we changed the auxiliary verb *was* from the active sentence to *were* in the passive sentence, because the auxiliary verb must agree in number with the subject of the sentence. The subject *classes* is plural, so the auxiliary must be plural.

Change the subject of the active sentence to the object of the preposition *by* in the passive sentence.

The classes were being taught by me.

Exceptions:

It rained last night. No passive.
It happened. No passive.

Verbs as Adjectives

We mentioned the grammatical and syntactic functions of a word and how the functions change when the positioning of a word changes in a sentence. Probably, the most confusing case in regard to that is the use of the verb as an adjective. The third form of the verb, the perfect form, is quite commonly used as an adjective, and it is seen in phrases and clauses, in the attributive and postpositional slots. One must watch very closely in order to ensure that he does not have a passive sentence when he thinks he has a subject, a verb, and an adjective after the linking verb, because the constructions are similar, some exactly alike. If you have questions concerning the relationship and the similarity between the passive and the present grammar point, refer back. Be assured that memorizing the verbs pays off, especially the irregular verbs, which is what we are primarily concerned with here. See appendix.

The mixture is shaken. (Shake, shook, shaken)

Usually, we can determine if a third form is an adjective two ways:

First, there is not an adverb in the structure. If the sentence read *The mixture is shaken daily*, then *shaken* would be part of the verb phrase, because *daily* would be an adverb of frequency indicating how often.

The horse is ridden.

Here, the logic is the same. If there were (I say *were*, because there is not: the condition is unreal, so we use *were* and not *was*) a *by* phrase that indicated passive voice or an adverb that modified the sentence, we would have definite information indicating the grammatical function of the word *ridden*. Therefore, it is wise to include indicators in the constructions of your sentences to avoid ambiguity.

The money is well spent. The well-spent dollar is the best one.

The car is hard-driven.

The words are hard-forgotten. The well-remembered man is a credit.

It is a hard-fought battle.

The fallen educator is a sad sight.

The proudly worn battle scar is scary.

The embattled factions reached a truce.

The well-meant word was taken wrongly.

Sentence Patterns

Causative Verb Constructions

Causative verbs are used when (1) a person influences another person to perform an action or (2) a person has something done to a thing. The three generally used causative verbs are *get*, *have*, and *make*.

Get = p + get + p + to + v1
Person + person (person = p)

I get Tom to write my letters.

He gets Tom to write his letters.

I got Tom to write my letters.

I have gotten Tom to write my letters.

I had gotten Tom to write my letters.

I am getting Tom to write my letters.

I will get Tom to write my letters.

I will be getting Tom to write my letters.

I will have gotten Tom to write my letters.

Get = p + get + t + v3
Person + get + thing (t) + v3

I get my car fixed.

I got my brakes repaired.

He gets his hair cut.

He is getting his hair cut.

He was getting his car inspected.

Ted will get his house built.

They will be getting the lawn trimmed.

They have gotten the leak plugged.

They had gotten the door made.

*He will get the cat to drink some milk.

(Exception: The cat is alive)

I will have gotten him arrested.

*With person + thing we can add the passive "*by* + noun."
She got the house estimated <u>by the tax man</u>.
Have = p + *have* + p + v1 or v-*ing*

I have him fix the lemonade.

I am having them study.

I am having my friend take notes.

I will have them eat early.

I have them eating early on Thursdays.

I have them reading.

I had him writing letters.

I will have already had them sweeping for one hour by 6:00.

P + have + t + v3
Person + have + thing + v3

I have the notes taken by Tom.

I have my house cleaned by the service.

He has his physical performed by Dr. Ben.

He is having his tonsils removed tomorrow by Dr. Fry.

He has had the panel reviewed by another agency.

He will have the test administered by the captain.

He will have had the procedure completed by tomorrow.

He had been having the treatment performed for over a year.

He will have been having his teeth cleaned for fifty minutes at 1:00.

$Make = \text{p} + make + \text{p} + \text{v1}$

$\text{P} + make + \text{t} + \text{v1}$

He makes his brother clean his car.

He is making his car clean. (He is cleaning the car himself.)

He made his car clean.

He is making the men run the track.

He was making the girls sing.

He had made them do pushups.

He made the car stop. (He physically stopped the car himself with the brake.)

The boy made the little girl scream.

He made the child steal.

He made the car be stolen. (It was his fault.)

The principal made the student be quiet.

The mother made the girl apologize.

Other Causative Patterns

He is forcing the employee to work.

He forced the men to eat.

The dictator ordered the men imprisoned.

He wanted the animal slaughtered.

He wanted the animals sleeping.

He will force them to wait.

He made them wait.

He is making them study.

He caused them to wait.

He is causing the orders to be rescinded.

He orders the insurgents drugged.

He insisted the men be bound.

They were insisting they be released.

They demanded to be ransomed.

They demanded the men be set free.

They were ordered killed.

They were to be killed.

The causative verb patterns are important, because logical fallacies spring up here. Also, to read a complicated text, one should be familiar with the patterns.

For, Since, Ago

These are used to show the relationship between an action and a time frame.

Patterns:

For: S–V–*for*–length of time (countable time)

Since: S–V–*since*–specific time (requires perfect aspect)

Ago: S–V–length of time (countable time)

For

Length of time includes minutes, hours, days, weeks, months, and years.

Tenses disallowed: simple present with a linking verb.

I am here for two hours. (colloquial only)

<u>Simple present</u>: I exercise for two hours daily.

<u>Present progressive</u>: I am writing for two hours daily.

<u>Simple past</u>: I rode for one hour to get here.

<u>Past progressive</u>: I was singing for years.

<u>Past perfect</u>: I had worked there for a year before the accident.

<u>Past perfect progressive</u>: I had been running for twenty minutes.

<u>Present perfect</u>: I have been here for six months.

<u>Present perfect progressive</u>: I have been learning for years.

<u>Simple future</u>: I will be there for a month.

<u>Future progressive</u>: I will be studying for the next week.

<u>Future perfect progressive</u>: I will have been reading for twenty years

next April.

Future perfect: I will have exercised for one hour by the time you arrive.

Since

Indicates the starting point/time of an action. The specific time indicates time, day, date, month, and year (or time specified in a clause).

Simple present: Disallowed

Present progressive: Disallowed

Simple past: Disallowed

Past progressive: Disallowed

Past perfect: I had worked there since May.

Past perfect progressive: I had been running since 8:00.

Present perfect: I have been here since 1997.

Present perfect progressive: I have been learning since I was a child.

Simple future: Disallowed

Future progressive: Disallowed

Future perfect progressive: Disallowed

Future perfect: Disallowed

Ago

The adverbial *ago* requires that one of the verbs in the verb phrase be in the past. Time includes minutes, hours, days, weeks, months, and years.

Simple present: Disallowed.

Present progressive: Disallowed

Simple past: I hurt myself one day ago.

Past progressive: I was reading an hour ago.

Past perfect: I had worked there since May.

Past perfect progressive: I had been running until the accident a year ago.

Present perfect: Disallowed

Present perfect progressive: Disallowed

Simple future: Disallowed

Future progressive: Disallowed

Future perfect progressive: Disallowed

Future perfect: Disallowed

The use of *since* always requires the perfect aspect (time relationship). The use of *ago* always requires a form of a past tense.

If you learn "embedding," which is described in the following section, you can read almost anything. This is the road to fluency in reading and writing.

Embedding

Embedding is a broad term used to refer to a clause within a clause, which we covered in part under relative clauses. The relative clauses are easy to see, because the presence of a *wh-* word (*who, what, where, when, why* [*how*]) indicates the probability of an additional clause in the superstructure. Further analysis is necessary to observe additional constructions that are highly common in academic settings. Students particularly have problems with readings such as philosophical discourses, scientific materials, and religious writings, which often have long, complicated structures similar to those included herein. In addition, to vary sentence structure, write about literature, and present your ideas effectively and interestingly, it is necessary to know the grammatical constructions. The first part, "Syntactic Positions," covers general positions of clauses that are subjects, IOs, and DOs in the sentence. The second part, "Complements," renames these words in sentences that function as subjects, IOs, and DOs.

Syntactic Positions

Subject

The labels are above the sentences. Underlined is the complete subject. For now, just think of the important information: it's the skeleton.

          S   V SC
A man (walking late at night) is not safe.

          S   Aux V Adv Adv
To see (the one you love die) can hurt very deeply.

<pre>
                    S   V   DO
Learning (to drive a car in the snow at night) confuses young people.
</pre>

<pre>
                      S   V   SC
That (we should have taken a different route) is an understatement.
</pre>

<pre>
                S   V   DO
Saying (you would have known better) angers me.
</pre>

<pre>
                   S   V   SC
The matter (that we discussed yesterday morning) is pending.
</pre>

<pre>
                 S   V SC
What you said (about my friends being infantile) is a lie.
</pre>

<pre>
                 S   V   DO
Where you go (after work with your friends) puzzles me.
</pre>

<pre>
                   S   V   SC
Swimming (around with a cut in shark-infested water) is really stupid.
</pre>

The dotted line indicates the simple subject; the underlined structure is the complete subject, and the *S* indicates the simple subject if we can go so far as to narrow it down to one word and still understand the sentence.

Direct Object

<pre>
S Aux   V   DO
I do not know <u>what he sees in the girl down the street</u>.
</pre>

<pre>
S V   DO
I think <u>that he is one of the lowest forms of life on this planet</u>.
</pre>

<pre>
S   V   DO
He said <u>he was going to try to find the prettiest girl to take to the dance</u>.
</pre>

S V   DO
I hate (that) <u>tomorrow is the day that we will both be walking away from this</u>.

S V   IO   DO
I stated to the policeman (that) <u>going to the store was necessary for baby</u>
<u>formula and diapers</u>.

S   V   DO
She thought <u>her life was taking a new turn with the money from the set-</u>
<u>tlement</u>.

      S   V   Do
The boy wondered <u>if God placed him here for his parents' joy</u>.

        S   V   DO
The flagman hit <u>the dog walking under the bridge</u>.

Tip: Look for the action verb. The entity receiving the action is the DO–usually.

Indirect Objects

S V   IO   DO
I gave <u>whoever he was</u> my assistance.

S V   IO   DO
I said <u>to whomever the little girl had hit</u> that they must come and report it.

S V   IO   DO
I gave <u>the little boy riding the bicycle</u> my stern disapproval.

S V   DO   IO
I said, "Don't return here or I'll be upset" <u>to the persistent salesman</u>.

Grammar Note

```
S  V                    IO                      DO
```
I told the man sitting at the bus stop that I would be right back.

NOTE: *If we are speaking to people, use the following patterns with* tell/told *and* say/said: Tell/Told: *S–tell/told–IO–DO (Do not use the word* to.)

Say/Said: S–say/said + *to* + IO + DO.
Say/Said: S–say/said + DO + *to* + IO.

```
S   V                   DO                      IO.
```
I handed the big case of beautiful Afghan flowers to the little boy.

```
      S        V        DO                      IO
```
The big man pushed the handful of money toward the lady in the box.

```
                              S                 V  DO  IO
```
The fat, old, lazy homeless man who was at the station gave a letter to me.

Recall that we said the best way to learn grammar and to learn to write is to look at the position of something in the text. By finding the subject and the verb of the sentence, you enable yourself to notice constructions in the structure that are not really necessary. Earlier we learned that transitions take us from one idea to the next, from sentence to sentence, and from paragraph to paragraph; there are always words in a sentence that do the same thing. For example, to see two nouns next to each other may mean that one is the start of a phrase or clause that renames the phrase or clause before it. Also, we know that most sentences have a subject and a verb, so to see two sets of verb phrases in a sentence means that there are probably two clauses, because most clauses have a subject and a verb.

Complements

Subject

```
                              S                          V   SC
```
The man, the one who was being chief officer for the day, is always
<u>a real headache</u>.

```
S  V                    SC
```
I am <u>the man writing the letters for all the students</u>.

```
  S        V                    SC
```
She seems to be <u>the one who started all of the problems</u>.

```
S      V    SC
```
She appeared tired, worn-out, and ready to go home.

Direct Object

```
  S  aux    V       DO                      O comp.
```
He was crowned Mr. Olympia, <u>the possessor of the most symmetrical body
in the world</u>.

```
  S    V    DO                  O comp (OC)
```
They made him the most feared leader in the whole Western world.

```
S    V    DO                       OC
```
I slugged the man, <u>the one being the most obnoxious pest at the party</u>.

```
S  V    DO                    OC
```
I made her <u>my wife, the partner who would share my life forever</u>.

```
S        V     DO        OC
```
I killed the dog that was eating the chickens in the pasture.

```
       S   V    DO                    OC
```
She saw the man that had plundered her cookie jar.

Indirect Object

```
S  V    DO                    IO                         IO  comp.
```
I gave the thing to the man wearing the big overcoat, <u>the one coughing</u>.

```
S  V    DO    IO              IO comp.
```
I gave the coat to the boy, <u>the one waving at us</u>.

```
       S      V    DO    IO                    IO comp.
```
The man wrote the letter for the boy <u>who was sick in the hospital</u>.

```
         S       V DO    IO                    IO comp.
```
The professor said hello to the man <u>who had wrecked the bus</u>.

```
S  V    DO        IO              IO comp.
```
I shovel the snow for the lady <u>who attends my church</u>.

The IOs in these sentences are technically the objects of the prepositions to and for, but we will view them according to the function in the sentence. Therefore, we will call them IOs.

The IO can usually be moved to the final position in the sentence and be preceded by the word to or for, depending on the construction. See grammar note above. Further, the complement can be realized by a noun phrase with a noun as headword or by a relative pronoun.

We will explore complements and clauses shortly. Complements can be realized by other constructions, as well.

Embedding Construction: *Who (Whom), Whose, What, Why, Where, When, How*

Three definite patterns emerge in this construction, each taking different syntactic functions. Numbers 1 and 2 are statements, and number 3 is an interrogative:

1. S–V–Question Word–S–V
2. S–V–Q. Word–(*to*)–V
3. Operator (auxiliary verb)–S–V–Q. Word–(S)–(V)

NOTE: *The words in parentheses are optional; therefore, we may have several patterns in number 3.*

Category 1

1. He knows who(m) the boy likes.
2. He knows whose cat this is. Note: We have an extra noun after *whose*.
3. I saw what you did.
4. I understand why she left.
5. He saw where the cow went.
6. I told you when the man arrived.
7. I do not understand how the train operates.

Category 2

1. I can't think of whom to call. I know who is here.
2. *I saw the girl whose mother won the race. S–V–Whose–S–V: Exception.*
3. I couldn't see what jumped. I felt what moved.
4. He said why to come early.
5. I know where to go.
6. I learned when to shut up
7. I know how to ski.

Category 3

1. Did you see who(m)?
2. Did you see who was here?
3. Do you know it was?
4. Do you know whose scarf it was?
5. Can they see what it hit?
6. Could you tell me why you went there?
7. Does he know where we went?
8. Can you tell me when the plane arrives?
9. Do you know how to solve the problem?

As with the pods, we can add to these constructions, and, of course, we can take away from them. To understand the basic elements of grammar, look at the constructions. Patterns emerge. By now, you are beginning to understand the structures within the structures. There may be several subjects in a sentence, each within a clause of its own, all fitting together to fit into its own syntactic slot in the superstructure. Understanding this enables one to look over his own papers and catch those costly mistakes that previously he would not have recognized.

We have now completed a general overview of syntactic constructions, referring to subjects, objects, and complements. We must now look further into the specific types of phrases and clauses and see how they can function in these syntactic positions.

Noun Phrases

A noun phrase consists of the headword, which is usually a noun or a word that is functioning like a noun, and the article that is situated before it, plus all of its modifiers (adjectives).

As Subject

<u>The big bully</u> ate the candy.
Det. Adj. S/N

It can consist of the possessive, hereafter referred to as the genitive.

S/N = the word that is the subject of the sentence; N = the part of speech that the subject is realized by.

The big bully's brother ate the candy.
Det. Adj. Adj./N S/N

The big brother of the bully ate the candy.
Det. Adj. S/N prep + Obj = PP: This is the inverted genitive realized by a prepositional phrase.

The big brother's running was excellent.
Det. Adj. Adj/N S/gerund

The running of the big brother was excellent.
Det. S/gerund + PP————————-.

Noun Phrase as an Adjective Describing the Subject

A beer mug is thick
Det. Adj/N S/n

An exam day is hectic.
Det. Adj/N S/n

Noun Phrase Realized by an Adjective as Headword of the Phrase

The decrepit fall often.
Det. S/adj.

The old and decrepit need help.
Det. S/adj S/adj

The sickly old and decrepit need guidance.
Det. adj/adj S/adj S/adj

The sentence above has two adjectives that act as nouns in order to function as the subjects of the sentence. The word *sickly* is an adverb and an adjective. Here, it is in the form of an adverb, because usually an adverb describes an adjective.

Definitions:

Verbal—A form of a verb that does not function as a verb: *The boiling milk is best*. Here, the word *boiling* functions as an adjective to describe the word *milk*. The verbal is also referred to as a participle. *Boiling* is the present <u>participle,</u> *boiled* is the past participle, and so forth.

Adjectival—A word, clause, or phrase functioning as an adjective: *The <u>brick</u> house is solid. Brick* is a noun, but it acts like an adjective in this sentence.

Adverbial—A word, clause, or phrase that functions as an adverb: broadly, it tells where, when, why, how, and to what degree.

NOTE: *These definitions above apply to words, phrases, and clauses.*

Noun Phrase Realized by Verb as Headword

<u>Running hard</u> is good for the young man.
S/V Adv

<u>Hardly running</u> is not a good training practice.
(*hardly* = little in amount [adverb])
Adv/adv S/V

<u>Crashing violently against the wall</u> is not an option.
S/V Adv PP = adverbial (tells) therefore describes.

Noun Phrase Realized by Adverb as Headword

<u>Violently</u> is the way he handled it.
S/adv

<u>Thrashingly</u> was the method by which they were controlled.
S/adv

Noun Phrase Realized by a Preposition

Under the table is no place to be.
S/prep + obj = PP

Below is not the position to have.
S/prep

Noun Phrase as Direct Object

I hate <u>the cloudy weather</u>.
Adj DO/N

I picked <u>the luscious berries</u>.
Det. Adj DO/N

Noun Phrase Realized by Verb

I would rather have <u>the beating</u>.
Det. DO/V/gerund

He saw <u>the ship's sinking</u>.
Det. Adj/N DO/gerund

He saw <u>the sinking of the ship</u>.
Det. DO prep + N = PP (adjectival)

Noun Phrase Realized by an Adjective

I hate <u>the filthy and the putrid</u>.
Det. DO/adj DO/adj

We learned <u>the unlearnable and the impossible</u>.
Det. DO/adj DO/adj

Noun Phrase Realized by an Adverb = Needs Linking Verb for the Common Usage

Noun Phrase Realized by a Prepositional Phrase = Needs Linking Verb for Common Usage

It is obvious how the patterns begin to form. Most words step out of their grammatical function when repositioned syntactically. Therefore, to quickly recapitulate, we have discussed the following structures:

In the subject position, a noun phrase is usually realized by:
Noun
Verb
Adjective
Adverb
Preposition

In the DO position, a noun phrase is usually realized by:
Noun
Verb
Adjective

Noun Phrase as IO

Noun Phrase Realized by Noun

I gave the little red balloon <u>to the boy</u>.
Prep + obj = PP

See note above; PP also serves as the IO.

I forfeited my band <u>to my friend</u>.
Prep + obj = PP

I handed <u>the professor</u> my paper.
IO (no prep)

NOTE: *There is rarely a preposition inside the syntactic structure when dealing with an IO, except for certain verbs. However, when placed at the end of the clause, the IO almost always is preceded by* to *or* for.

Noun Phrase Realized by Verbal

I turned him <u>to judging</u>. *Note: Unable to invert the syntax.*
Prep + obj = PP = O/gerund

I warned Tom <u>against gambling</u>. *Note: Unable to invert the IO and DO.*
Prep + obj = PP = O/gerund

Noun Phrase Realized by Adjective

I give <u>the young</u> my advice.
Det. IO/Adj

I gave my time <u>to the sad</u>.
Prep + IO/adj

These are easily inverted, especially with the verb *give*.

We have begun to examine structures that exercise worlds of different functions as they move around in the superstructure. Therefore, I must make some distinctions. More than one phrase can act simultaneously in a syntactic position. For example:

<u>The big, fat, ugly</u> *bear* ate the lunch basket.

The big, fat, ugly bear = the complete subject
Bear = the simple subject

We basically have two phrases together in the subject's position: an adjective phrase and a noun phrase. The adjective phrase is underlined, and the noun phrase is bolded. However, the complete noun phrase is the same as the complete subject, because all of the adjectives are pointing to the noun as their leader. They describe ***the bear.*** Although we could possibly stretch the availability of some constructions in certain positions syntactically, at times, some of these are not widely used. As a result, many possible constructions will be omitted, or, if a certain phrase acts in a subordinate position to the complete phrase in which it is included, the construction most typically used in the same manner will be demonstrated. There are many included in these diagrams. We will point out the grammatical peculiarities in addition to other features, which should be taken into account.

Noun Phrase as Complement: Subject Complement

Noun Phrase Realized by a Noun

My friend is <u>the baker</u>.
Det. SC/N

He is <u>my friend</u>.
Poss. pro. SC/N

Noun Phrase Realized by a Verbal

They are <u>the beaten</u>.
Det. SC/V3

The subservient are <u>whipped</u>.
SC/V3

Noun Phrase Realized by an Adjective

He is <u>the first</u>.
Det. SC/adj

They are <u>the last</u>.
Det. SC/adj

Noun Phrase Realized by an Adverb

The synonym is <u>atrociously</u>.
SC/Adv

The adverb is <u>stunningly</u>.
SC/Adv.

Noun Phrases Realized by Prepositions

This is at <u>the bottom</u>.
Det. SC/ Prep (N)

Noun Phrases as Complement of Direct Object (DOc)

Noun Phrase Realized by Noun

They appointed him <u>the chief</u>.
Det. DOc/N

He named him <u>the leader</u>.
Det. DOc/N

Noun Phrase Realized by Verbal

They killed the worst, <u>the bludgeoned</u>.
Det. DOc/V3

They expelled the men, <u>the disgraced</u>.
Det. DOc/V3

Noun Phrase Realized by an Adjective

He thought her <u>beautiful</u>.
DOc/adj

He considered it <u>awful</u>.
DOc/adj

He called him <u>ugly</u>.
DOc/adj

Noun Phrase Realized by Adverb

He termed the approach <u>as cautiously</u>.
Det/adv DOc/adv

(It was the term/definition he gave to describe the approach.)

He redescribed it <u>as surprisingly</u>.
Adv DOc/Adv

Noun Phrase Realized by Preposition

He defined his life <u>as being at the very top</u>.
Det/Adv;   pres.   part.

Prep + det + adj/adv + prep/n = DOc

This construction seems complicated, but it is very common, especially in speech. However, we can view the entire complement as an adjectival, one that acts as an adjective when it is not realized by an adjective, much like the verbal, a form of a verb that functions as an adjective.

Noun Phrases as Complement of Indirect Object (IOc)

Noun Phrase Realized by Noun

He gave her, <u>the girl</u>, his coat.
        Det Ioc/N

He handed it to her, <u>his friend</u>.
        Poss pro. IOc/N

Noun Phrase Realized by Verbal

I gave respect to her, <u>the dethroned</u>.
        Det IOc/V3

We gave honor to the men, the fallen.
        Det IOc/V3

Noun Phrase Realized by Adjective

We give respect to the marines, <u>the bold</u>.
        Det IOc/Adj

We give a high place to ourselves, the free.
        Det IOc/Adj

Noun Phrase Realized by Adverb
We looked at the DOc realized by an adverb phrase, but this is highly uncommon as an IOc. Usually this construction requires a headword formed from a different part of speech.

Noun Phrase Realized by Preposition

He gave his time <u>for/to the underprivileged</u>.
Prep + det + N = IOc (Not common = under [prep] + adj = N

Up until this point, we have examined how noun phrases can be realized by (1) noun, (2) verbal, (3) adjectival, (4) adverbial, and (5) prepositional phrases. Also, we have seen how they function syntactically as (a) subjects, (b) IOs, (c) DOs, and (d) complements that rename a, b, and c in a sentence. Instead of taking this same approach with verb phrases, I will set forth some of the ways in which the verb phrase may function. Here, verbal is usually v3.

Noun Phrase Realized by a Verbal
Subject

The <u>best written</u> (paper) will receive the prize.
<u>Adv + V3</u>
S

NOTE: Best *is part of the compound subject (two words that form one; therefore, it is hyphenated, which is very common when a word does not function as its normal part of speech syntactically). Here, the noun that acts as the headword in this phrase is omitted; this omission is termed* ellipsis. *The omitted word is shown in parentheses. Without the word* paper, *the underlined word becomes the subject of the sentence.*

The well-refined have a presence about them.
Adv Adj/Verbal

Adjective

The <u>acclaimed</u> man won the admiration of many.
Adj/Verbal

She is a <u>censured</u> woman.
Adj/V3

Adverb

He wrote fast-paced.
Adv/adv + V3 = Adv

Things went <u>swimmingly</u>.
Pres prog verb + ly = adv

Adjective Phrase

Adjective Phrases as Subject

Adjective Phrase Realized by Noun

The <u>Mercedes</u> (car) is well built.
S/N-adj (S/N)

The <u>American</u> (man) is strong.
S/N-adj (S/N)

A (stucco) <u>house</u> is cheap. Or: A house of stucco . . .
Adj/N S/N

We cannot write *A stucco is cheap.* So, *stucco* is the complete adjective phrase that modifies the headword of the noun phrase *stucco house. Stucco* is a noun, but it functions as an adjective when it precedes another noun. Most often, a noun that functions as an adjective cannot do so unless it is positioned before the noun it describes or immediately thereafter. Sometimes, the two nouns are interchangeable. At times, we make it possessive. Examples: house frame

The doorknob, the door's knob (Not: the knobdoor or the knob's door), the paper shredder, the paper's shredder, the cement mix, the mix of cement, the boy wonder, the wonder boy.

Adjective Phrases Realized by Verbals

A <u>blurted</u> word has consequences.
Adj/v3 S

The blurted has consequences.
S/v3

Notice how the word changed functions when we took out the noun *word*.

Adjective Phrases Realized by Adjectives

<u>Being popular</u> is not a bad thing.
Verbal + adj = S

> *Some adjectives are somewhat active in the sense that a person, or a living thing with a will, can change behavior when the adjective is used to describe the noun in question. For example:* He is being nice. She is being courteous. *I would not, on the other hand, write* The storm is being bad. *The storm has no ability to will or desire itself to change. Therefore, we write* The storm is bad.

<u>Being the best</u> is not that important.
Verbal Det Adj = S

<u>(Being) Sweet</u> is a wonderful attribute.
S/Adj

<u>Sweets</u> will rot one's teeth.
S/Adj + s = plural

Some adjectives as nouns are commonly declined in terms of singular and plural. This is true in colloquial usage.

Adjective Phrases Realized by Adverbs

The <u>smartly run</u> race is the best.
Adj/adv adj/V3 = adj. with verbal as headword

The <u>well-behaved</u> child is a blessing.
Adv adj/V3 = adj.

Adjective Phrase Realized by a Preposition

Under-the-table dealings are not tolerated.
Prep det obj = PP
Pp = adj. Describing the S/gerund

He is a behind-the-back operator.
Prep-det-obj = PP = adj desc. SC

Adjective Phrases as DO:

Adjective Phrases Realized by Noun N = Adj (compound)

I hate <u>surprise parties</u>.
Adj/n DO/n
_____DO_____

I bought a pretty <u>ashtray</u>
Adj/N DO/N

It is common to compound a noun and the noun it describes.

Adjective Phrases Realized by Verbals

I detest the <u>unreserved</u> stranger.
Adj/verbal

If we take out the headword stranger, unreserved *can function as the DO.*

I use only <u>distilled</u> (water).
Adj/Verbal: Can be DO without water.

Adjective Phrases Realized by Adjectives

I took in the old (people).
DO/adj

We help the <u>meek</u> (animals).
DO/adj

Adjective Phrase Realized by Adverb

I caught <u>the furtively thrown (glance)</u>.
Adj/adv + V3 or DO/adv + V3

I shunned the <u>previously embraced (ideals)</u>.
Adj/adv + V3 or DO/adv + V3

With most of the constructions we have seen involving an Adv + V3, the function can be twofold:

1. The Adv + V3 without noun = DO (nominal function regardless of syntactic positioning).
2. The Adv + V3 + N = (Adv + V3 = adjectival function)

It is important to notice the function a phrase takes on in its place in the sentence, because the presence of an additional word or the loss thereof changes meanings and functions, not to mention punctuation in certain structures.

Adjective Phrase Realized by Prepositional Phrase

I always assist <u>the down-and-out</u> (people).
Adj/prep + prep or DO/prep + prep

He employs <u>the over and under (style)</u>.
Adj/prep + prep or DO/prep + prep

Adjective Phrases as IO

Adjective Phrases Realized by Nouns

I traded John to the <u>ball (team)</u>.
                    Adj/N

I saved some cake for the <u>baseball</u> players.
                       Adj/N

Adjective Phrases Realized by Verbals

The money is also given <u>to the undeserving (population)</u>.
                    IO/verbal or adj/verbal

The manager gave the position <u>to the best-suited (applicant)</u>.
                       IO/verbal or adj/verbal

Both examples can be the IO without the inclusion of the final noun.

Adjective Phrases Realized by Adjectives

I lent encouragement <u>to the blind (students)</u>.
IO/adj or adj/adj

I taught a lesson <u>to the stupid (animals)</u>.
IO/adj or adj/adj

Both examples can be the IO without the final noun.

Adjective Phrases Realized by Adverb

The town money was allotted <u>for the slowly developed (section)</u>.
Adv + V3 = adj

He waged an <u>effectively run</u> (campaign).
Adv V3 = adj

Adjective Phrases Realized by Prepositions

He delivered the speech to the <u>in-your-face</u> generation.
Prep poss pro = PP = adj

They finalized an <u>under-the-counter</u> proposition.
Prep det N = PP = adj

CHAPTER SIX

Odds and Ends

Irregular Verbs list

Forms

Verb1 (v1) Base	verb2 (v2) Simple Past	verb3 (v3) Perfect
is, am, are	was, were	been
become	became	become
begin	began	begun
blow	blew	blown
bring	brought	brought
build	built	built
buy	bought	bought
catch	caught	caught
choose	chose	chosen
come	came	come
do	did	done
draw	drew	drawn
drink	drank	drunk
drive	drove	driven
eat	ate	eaten

| Verb1 (v1) | verb2 (v2) | verb3 (v3) |
Base	Simple Past	Perfect
fall	fell	fallen
feel	felt	felt
fight	fought	fought
find	found	found
fly	flew	flown
forget	forgot	forgotten
get	got	gotten
give	gave	given
go	went	gone
grow	grew	grown
have	had	had
hear	heard	heard
hold	held	held
keep	kept	kept
know	knew	known
leave	left	left
lend	lent	lent
lose	lost	lost
make	made	made
mean	meant	meant
meet	met	met
pay	paid	paid
read	read	read
ride	rode	ridden
ring	rang	rung
run	ran	run
say	said	said
see	saw	seen
sell	sold	sold
send	sent	sent
shake	shook	shaken
shoot	shot	shot
sing	sang	sung
sit	sat	sat

Verb1 (v1)	verb2 (v2)	verb3 (v3)
Base	**Simple Past**	**Perfect**
sleep	slept	slept
speak	spoke	spoken
spend	spent	spent
stand	stood	stood
steal	stole	stolen
take	took	taken
teach	taught	taught
tear	tore	torn
tell	told	told
think	thought	thought
throw	threw	thrown
understand	understood	understood
wear	wore	worn
win	won	won
write	wrote	written
cost	cost	cost
cut	cut	cut
hit	hit	hit
hurt	hurt	hurt
put	put	put
shut	shut	shut
set	set	set

Verbs + Gerund/Infinitive

Use a Gerund after the Following Verbs
(gerund = verb + -ing; example: enjoy walking)
Enjoy

Mind

Finish

Keep

Be accustomed to

Look forward to

Am used to (adj)
Appreciate
Avoid
Consider
Dislike
Delay
Deny
Help
Mention
Miss
Postpone
Quit
Regards
Risk
Suggest
Understand

Use a Gerund after the Following Prepositions

Of	He is afraid of flying.
After	After working, he took a shower.
By	He lost weight by exercising.
For	He got a badge for camping.
About	We learned about skydiving.
In	He is interested in writing.
On	They insist on coming.
Before	I eat before exercising.
While	I smoke while watching movies.
From	I was delivered from smoking.
Upon	Upon returning, he was arrested.
When	When arriving, call your mother.
While	He got hurt while playing.
With	With exercising, losing weight is easy.
Within	He was within shouting distance.
Without	He was speeding without realizing it.

Use a Gerund or Infinitive after These Verbs (infinitive = to + v1; example: intend to walk)

Intend, start, begin, continue, stop, cease, leave, remember, like, love, hate, study, prefer, forget, agree, try, admit, propose

Two-Part Verbs

Account for	**To explain the reason**
Call up	To telephone
Call down	To be angry with, to correct in public
Call in	To require someone to see you, to ask for assistance
Call on	To go see a person, to ask for assistance
Call for	To ask for something to be given
Call off	To cancel
Call out	To announce, to yell
Call over	To announce using an intercom or machine
Catch up	To get to the same place of progress after being behind
Catch on (to)	To understand
Check in	To get a room at a hotel, to make your official presence known, to call home to make sure things are OK
Check out	To leave a hotel, to inspect or examine, to borrow a book from a library, to find out the truth
Check up	To get an examination from a doctor, dentist, etc.
Check up on	To see if things are OK
Clear up	To become nice and sunny (e.g., the weather), to solve a problem
Clear out	To leave a place taking the possessions, to delete information from a computer or file
Cut in (on)	To interrupt, to break in a line before the person ahead
Cut off	To stop service, to cut a piece of something, to stop someone in the middle of a sentence
Cut away	To trim the excess from
Cut out	To stop a habit, to cut a paper or cloth with scissors
Cut down (on)	To reduce, to lessen in amount

Account for	**To explain the reason**
Cut up	To cut into small pieces
End up	To finish, to obtain a final result
Figure (out)	To think, to solve a problem, to find an answer
Figure up	To find the total (e.g., of a bill)
Figure in	To think of all the things that must be included
Go over	To review, to go to a place
Go along with	To agree
Get along with	To interact with a person politely
Get over	To heal from a sickness, to recover from a bad time or sadness
Get under	To take shelter, to support an idea or person
Go on	To continue
Get around	To go near
Get on with	To continue
Get by with	To do something without punishment, to use carefully due to a small supply
Give in	To agree to do something you do not want to do
Give up	To give a thing you do not want to give, to surrender
Give out	To allow someone to have something free, to get tired and stop
Give away	To allow someone to take something free, to divulge (tell) information
Hand over	To give something that does not belong to you
Hand in	To give assignment to the teacher
Hand out	To give something to a person, to distribute to people
Hand down	To give something to someone in your family (i.e., a younger person gets something of value from the older person)
Jot down	To quickly write something
Keep out	To prevent from entering
Keep up	To make progress at the same rate as others, to continue
Keep on	To continue
Keep in	To not allow to go outside
Keep away	To not go near

Account for	**To explain the reason**
Keep at it	To continue to try something difficult
Look up	To find information (e.g., in a book)
Look up to	To admire, to respect
Look to	To use something or someone for an example
Look at	To watch, to observe
Look in on	To see if things are OK, to see personally
Look out	To be careful
Look after	To assist a person, to maintain something
Look over	To review
Look around	To see an area (e.g., as a tourist)
Look for	To search for something or someone, to wait for
Make out	To see clearly, to recognize, to get the final result
Make up	To lie, to imagine, to become friends again after a fight, to take a test or do work that was missed
Make over	To create something again, to be better
Mess up	To make an error, to ruin something
Mess around	To waste time, to be unfaithful
Pick out	To choose, to select
Pick up	To go and get, to get something that was dropped
Pick on	To start problems with a weaker person again and again
Pick over	To look at a pile of things very slowly to decide what you want
Point out	To indicate, to show
Put on	To wear something
Put off	To delay
Put up	To invite someone to sleep at your house
Put up with	To tolerate, to endure
Put out	To set outside, to extinguish a fire, to bother someone
Run into	To see someone by chance
Run short of	To run low on a supply
Run out of	To use up a supply
Run up	To cause the cost (e.g., of a bill) to get higher
Run away	To leave a problem
Run over	To hit with a vehicle, to use someone wrongly

Account for	To explain the reason
Take over	To get control
Take on	To acquire
Take up	To start something enjoyable, to shorten (e.g., pants)
Take in	To help someone or something by allowing the person or thing to live with you
Take around	To show someone a place, to give a tour
Take out	To go on a date, to buy food at the restaurant and take it
Take apart	To disassemble
Try on	To wear and see if something is the right size
Try out	To see if something is acceptable
Turn out	To get a result
Turn up	To increase the volume, to arrive unexpectedly, to show evidence, to find out secret information
Turn down	To refuse, to reject, to reduce the volume
Turn in	To go to bed, to report information or something that is found to the police, to give an assignment to the teacher
Turn around	To position the body or face in a different direction, to discontinue certain actions
Turn over	To place a thing in the opposite direction
Used to	To have done something in the past but to have quit
Use up	To finish the supply of something
Wind up	To finish, to become angry
Wind away	To continue a task that is boring
Work (it) out	To solve a problem
Work out	To exercise
Work up (to)	To slowly try to achieve something
Work up	To become angry, to make something
Work over	To do something again to make better, to beat someone
Work around	To avoid an existing problem
Work under	To work despite the existence of a problem

More on Adjectives

The following adjectives do not take gradation: *perfect, real, utter, only, same, precise, exact, pregnant, dead, alive, rotund, afraid.*

Rules:

1. If an adjective has seven letters or more, modify it with *more* or *most*. Exceptions: *wealthy, naughty, healthy, handsome, obscure, handsome, friendly.*

2. If the adjective is formed by adding *-ed* or *-ing,* do not add *-er* or *-est* to make the comparative or superlative. Modify it with *more* or *most*.

3. With gradable adjectives, if the adjective ends in *y,* change *y* to *i,* and add *-er* or *-est.* Examples: *friendlier, happiest,* and *lonelier.*

4. Use *more* and *most* with adjectives ending in *ous.*

5. Do not pluralize an adjective that has been turned into a noun.

Example: Rich = rich people. Do not write *The riches live on the hill.*
Do write *The rich live on the hill.* (Better yet, write *The rich live next door.*)
Irregular gradation:
Little, less, least
Bad, worse, worst
Good, better, best
Far, farther/further, farthest/furthest
Some suffixes for adjectives:
-al: adjectival, lexical
-ic: phonemic, chiropractic, hectic
-like: childlike
-en: wooden
-ish: boyish
-able, -ible: retractable
-ful: wonderful
-ous: continuous

More on Nouns

NOTE: *Some of these words fall into both categories.*

Use singular verbs:

Oxygen, garbage, clothing, food, trash, underwear, Tupperware, sheep, hatred, eyewear, hair, air, coffee, deceit, shyness, truthfulness, honesty, beauty

Use plural verbs:

Sheep, foods, monies, peoples, coffees, British, Portuguese, woods, scissors, and pants

F changes to *v* in the plural:

Leaf, loaf, roof, half, knife, calf, wolf, elf, shelf

To make a verb from these words, add *-e*.

Cloth, breath, wreath, sleuth

Homophones and Homonyms

Homophones

Homophones are words that are pronounced the same but have different spellings and different meanings.

See	With the eyes
Sea	The water
Site	A place
Sight	To see with the eyes
Sink	To not float
Sync	In harmony
Tail	The long thing on the end of a dog
Tale	A story
Die	To discontinue living
Dye	To change the color
Meat	Flesh
Meet	To see someone somewhere
Beet	A vegetable
Beat	To hit
Week	Seven days
Weak	Opposite of strong
Peer	Someone your age, a friend or colleague

Pier	A structure that extends from the land over the water
Bear	Animal
Bare	Uncovered
Way	Method, direction
Weigh	To determine the mass of using a scale
Slay	To kill
Sleigh	The thing Santa Claus rides on
Mail	Packages and letters sent through the postal service
Male	Opposite of *female*
Might	Model verb (You should know this one.)
Mite	A small insect
Sell	To make available for purchase
Sale	A place where people take things for others to buy and go to buy
Pray	To talk to God
Prey	Something—an animal, for example—that is hunted by another
For	Reason
Four	After three
Bored	Disinterested
Board	Food
Maul	Attack and hurt
Mall	Where my wife spends my money
Write	To put down by transcription
Right	Correct, opposite of left
Rome	City in Italy
Roam	To wander
Resend	To send again
Rescind	To repeal, to take back

Homonyms

Homonyms are words that have the same sound, the same spelling, and different meanings.

Hard	Difficult
Hard	Opposite of *soft*
Chief	Main

Chief	Leader
Spot	To see
Spot	A stain or dirty area
Die	To pass away
Die	Metal to cut holes
Sink	To submerge
Sink	A washbasin
Tail	To follow
Tail	The end of a piece of clothing
Drove	Past tense of *drive*
Drove	A flock
Mean	Expression of one's thoughts
Mean	Not nice

Grammar Exercises

Exercise 7.1

Directions: *Punctuate the following sentences.*

1. I did three things at the store I ate a sample of fruit I had an encounter with an old friend finally I ran into my boss

2. If I ever go to bed after midnight I usually wake up with a headache the next morning but I didnt this morning

3. She said that she was only looking for one thing at her new job money!

4. Most likely it will rain in the evening and we will have to cancel our plans for the trip the next day.

5. I think however the day may turn out to be nice because the weatherman said it will be sunny all weekend.

6. If I told you that I was a policeman would you respect me differently?

7. i bought some milk tea a big container of flour and some bread

8. although he really does not know his job they will keep him on board until the summer is over.

9. The professor quoted several things in his lecture first the Civil War was an economic one second he indicated that the migration forced the South to take a different approach to its economics and most importantly the outcome was a higher expanse of trade in the North.

10. Now I know you are a little leery of meeting new people but I want you to try and open up because we love you.

11. If I were a woman I think I would be just like me.

12. I dont want any candy and he doesnt want any either.

13. I cant have any coffee nor can I have tea after dinner.

14. He went to his mothers house then he went to the house.

15. He is to put it lightly a very rude person.

16. The man was according to the police a loner who had had a fight with the stores owner before closing time.

Exercise 7.2

Directions: *Punctuate the following sentences. Make all answers only one sentence.*

1. The girl the sister the mother and the boyfriend all were injured in the plane accident but thank God no one was killed.

2. Because he was my friend I did not say anything however I will say something next time because that behavior is totally unacceptable.

3. Since I was the fastest of the group the coach made me run more study harder material and clean his car every week.

4. I left early but if I want to get there in time I will have to hurry even more.

5. I talked with the man then I turned to the professor but Ill never carry on at least try not to two conversations at once again.

6. I came early so I could get a good seat.

7. When I was a kid i use to fly a kite weekly.

8. I wouldve found the keys but I got a call and you know how my mother talks.

EXERCISE 7.2

9. To win the game they cheated every chance they got.

10. Today I talked with Robbie ate lunch at the restaurant and went to a movie but believe me Im tired.

EXERCISE 7.3

Exercise 7.3

Directions: *Punctuate the following sentences.*
There may be several options. Correct all mistakes that you find.

1. I went to class and studied afterward then I went over to Toms restaurant and I met some of my classmates.

2. Slipping on the ice is never fun but unfortunately its a hazard of living in a cold part of the world then again Id rather live here than africa.

3. Call me crazy but i think that you should go the man and apologize after all you were in the wrong just as much as him.

4. do you think that youll ever have your own apartment i cant live like this anymore you know that youre not the easiest person to get along with.

5. i certainly understand when a man loses his desire to go to work but on the other hand i could never buy into the idea of quitting life completely.

6. If i were you I would try to fix my car before the cold weather sets in.

7. She strolled along the riverbank and eyed the horizon but nevertheless she was still lonely in that she had lost the one and only person she had ever trusted

8. stand straight now raise your left arm

9. If you my one and only friend were in trouble I would do all I could if possible to fix everything but only with you

10. The chief of the department who is also my friend told me three things the day was long today is good and he was tired

11. Bluntly put I couldnt have said it better myself because I am a believer in justice unlike you however you should never talk badly at least around those of us who do believe.

12. he said and i quote this is the best team ive ever seen

13. according to the doctor she could live but digest said and this is a quote there is a 90 percent success rate in women 30 to 40 years of age.

14. Once i was a young man but i aged as all before me have done.

15. If this world were mine i would feed the hungry shelter the homeless and find a way to better life at least i would certainly try.

16. To find a good bank takes tenacity skill and a lot of luck one can quit but hell never get what he wants so ask what you need to know

17. Therefore he was stranded moreover he had no money and no friends and he was a long way from home.

18. I received many things such as socks pants shirts but I liked to be honest the socks the black ones

19. I saw a good sport namely kickboxing but when i saw a guy get killed i stopped patronizing it altogether

20. My friend plays rugby the other plays nothing and the other sleeps all day.

21. Walking along the road he thought of life liberty and his happiness until he was flattened by a gust of wind then he only thought about according to him catching his breath.

22. Running the track can be good however it is exhausting especially on days when one is already tired but I digress

23. You know john ive always wanted to be the president of the u.s. but now im too old

24. She did three things she ate out she studied then she retired.

Exercise 7.4

Directions: *Choose the correct answer.*

1. Could you tell me_____?
a. what kind of drink she prefers
b. what kind of drink would she prefer
c. what kind of drinking would she prefer
d. what kind of drink does she prefer

2. If the boy had listened to me, _____
a. he would had have taken the job
b. he had have been taking the job
c. he would have taken the job
d. he would have been taken the job

3. She is _____. That is why I listen to her.
a. interest
b. interested
c. interesting
d. interests

4. The land _____ is located in the forest.
a. that my father bought it
b. which it my father bought
c. which my father has bought it
d. which has bought my father
e. which my father bought

5. A birthday present _____ by my wife.
a. was to me given
b. was me given
c. was given to me
d. was gaven me

6. _____ the manual, you must know English.
   a. To reading
   b. To have been read by
   c. To be read
   d. To read

7. Do all of the employees at work understand_____?
   a. why does the boss allow them to stay
   b. why does the boss allows them to stay
   c. why the boss he allows them to stay
   d. why the boss allows them to stay

8. The students have been waiting _____.
   a. since two hours
   b. since two hours ago
   c. for two hours ago
   d. for two hours

9. Amy would like to get a car, and _____.
   a. so do I
   b. so will I
   c. so I do, too
   d. so would I

10. I went to the store _____.
    a. so to get a coke.
    b. so I could get a coke
    c. to be getting a coke
    d. so to be getting a coke

11. It is freezing out here now. You must _____cold. Do you want my coat?
    a. get
    b. be get cold
    c. are getting
    d. be getting

EXERCISE 7.4

12. I would buy a Mercedes if the price _____. But, it is.
    a. wasn't so expensive
    b. isn't so expensive
    c. hadn't been so expensive
    d. weren't so expensive

13. John got Bob _____the car.
    a. Wash
    b. washing
    c. to wash
    d. to washed

14. If it _____ so gloomy, it would have been nice weather.
    a. wasn't
    b. hadn't been
    c. weren't
    d. isn't

15. _____is broken, can you call me instead?
    a. So my clock
    b. Because my clock
    c. Since my clock it
    d. So my clock it

16. The steak _____ was very tough.
    a. which we ordered it
    b. that we ordered it
    c. which one we ordered
    d. which we ordered

17. We tried _____, but to no avail.
    a. to be having the car fixed
    b. to have the car fixing
    c. to had the car fixed
    d. to have the car fixed

EXERCISE 7.4

18. _____ is very annoying.
   a. To be interrupting by someone
   b. Being interrupted by someone
   c. To interrupt by someone
   d. To have been interrupted by someone

19. Can you tell me _____?
a. where was he sitting
b. where was he sit
c. where he was sit
d. here he was sitting

EXERCISE 7.5

Exercise 7.5

Directions: *Change the following sentences from active to passive voice.*

1. The boys played football.
2. The army was flying helicopters over the base late at night.
3. The girls achieved the highest award given by the organization.
4. The baseball team won most of the games they played this year.
5. The jury decided the fate of the accused murderers.
6. The plane crashed in the Andes late last night.
7. No one survived the crash in the Andes last night.
8. The group of boys taunted the girls walking across the yard.
9. The kittens roamed about the yard playing.
10. The professor pounded the desk in frustration.
11. The teacher modeled his class after what he was taught.
12. The bear splashed through the stream clumsily.
13. The best student flunked the exam.
14. The girl perused the headlines for any word of snow.
15. The fat, old, ugly bear consumed the picnic.
16. Beside the road, a snake swallowed the mouse.

17. The regiment formed a battle line.
18. The ball hit the backboard and made a noise.
19. The policemen captured the murderer behind the station.
20. An old lady hobbled along the sidewalk.
21. A dog ripped open the sack when he smelled the meat.

Exercise 7.6

Directions: *Change from active to passive voice.*

1. Eating an apple is a noisy experience.
2. Along the highway, we encountered a wolf.
3. To sing a song helps the heart.
4. Singing achieves a merriment in the heart.
5. The old miser distributed ill will around his neighborhood.
6. The rotten apple stank.
7. The glisten of the lights made the car shine.
8. The car's brakes squeaked loudly as he applied them.
9. The cub pranced through its den.
10. The water made a trickling sound as it ran down the drain.
11. To win the game, the goalie cheated.
12. He repaired the copier.
13. He is eating dinner later now.
14. The lady tossed the ashtray into the receptacle.
15. The computer whirred when he turned it on.

Exercise 7.7

Directions: *Change the following sentence from active to passive, and punctuate it.*

The man wrapped the gift then he hid the bottle in the fireplace next the man threw out the extra paper finally he discarded the evidence

Exercise 7.8

Directions: *Find the independent clause and the dependent clause in each sentence. Mark the independent clause by underlining it, and write* IC. *Indicate the dependent clause by writing* DC. *Do not rely on ellipsis to make a clause.*

1. The man became extremely irritated when the little boy begged for candy.

2. Once, when I was just a small boy about five, my dad took me to the zoo.

3. I hate to eat and run, but I must inform you now, so you won't get angry later.

4. The man whom I always called my uncle was the guy whom they called Dewey.

5. As he learned later on in life, the things that come easy are not always the best things to have.

EXERCISE 7.8

6. <u>I think that running on an empty stomach is a bad idea</u>.

7. <u>The fat cat</u>, the one I caught eating out of the trash, <u>was run over</u>.

8. <u>The strange culture teaches a young man that he must adapt</u>.

9. <u>Eating after midnight must be terrible for the system</u>.

10. <u>Do you know if today is cold</u>?

EXERCISE 7.9

Exercise 7.9

Directions: *Identify the complete subject by underlining it.*

1. The old man down the street makes me very angry sometimes.

2. The little girl to whom you gave some candy is a good student.

3. The old, rickety truck blew up on the highway.

4. The stately living in homes lose their dignity if not treated wisely.

5. To lose at what you love the most crushes one after too many losses.

6. Running on a full tank of premium lessens the wear on an engine.

7. The administering of unlawful drugs without permission is a felony.

8. To slowly and painfully wither away is a fact of life.

9. Eating from the fruit of life sustains the health.

10. Evangelism in the West is on the rise.

11. "To rise with the chickens" is an old phrase.

12. I love my family.

Exercise 7.10

Directions: *Identify the subject complement by underlining it.*

1. He looks tired.

2. It seems awfully cold today.

3. The look in her eye was mesmerizing.

4. To doubt oneself is the ultimate insult.

5. Thinking of you only makes me free.

6. Arbitrarily making judgments is not a shrewd business practice.

7. I have over the course of time become a man.

8. He appears to be the steadiest person I know.

9. A catastrophic event seems to be almost life-sustaining.

10. To think that I almost lost is unthinkable.

EXERCISE 7.10

11. Mission Control is one of the largest and most comprehensive centers.

12. Walking alone late at night is certainly a chilling experience.

13. The order which came from above looked like a forged document.

14. Being tall and having a good wife and beautiful children is great.

15. To necessitate the arrival of reinforcements equals trouble.

16. "They call me trouble," is what he said.

17. My favorite pastime is probably going to the lake at sundown.

18. What he says and what he does are two totally separate things.

19. Finding all of these stupid, inane grammatical points is frustrating.

20. Walking for exercise became the one most tolerable exercise.

EXERCISE 7.11

Exercise 7.11

Directions: *Identify the direct object with* DO *and the indirect object with* IO.

1. I learned that we had issued him a book.

2. After receiving the answer, I passed it to the dean.

3. To give the book to them was a mistake.

4. I think you must learn to give your time more freely.

5. Understand the lesson, and you will succeed.

6. I had him administer the exam.

7. If you write the letter, I will take the money.

8. Did you tell him to sit down?

9. I learned the method in a short time.

10. Eat more fruit, and you will not be tired.

11. Can you say anything?

12. I did not think so.

13. If I say no, will you leave?

14. Write all the answers.

15. Where did you place the file?

16. I eat fish frequently, but I only told him the story yesterday.

17. Read the article to understand the meaning.

18. Pop that top, and we will celebrate.

19. I hate to wait.

20. He wants to leave.

21. I have a desire for tacos.

Exercise 7.12

Directions: *Gerunds and infinitives have three functions: (1) to act as the subject, (2) to act as the direct object, and (3) to indicate reason. Indicate* I *for infinitive and 1, 2, or 3 for function and* G *for gerund and 1, 2, or 3 for function.*

1. I am here for learning.

2. To learn, we must be prepared to study.

3. To regain the love of his life, the man learned to write poetry.

4. The purpose of writing is to communicate.

5. I have been waiting to speak with you.

6. In order to revive him, she administered mouth-to-mouth resuscitation.

7. She was afraid to go out at dawn.

8. I want to leave at noon.

9. I heard whispering over the phone.

10. Walking on ice can be dangerous.

11. I am learning to tread water.

12. To think of her made him crazy.

13. Reading is not the easiest thing sometimes.

14. If you are wanting to ride, meet me at 6:00 to go over there.

15. Learning to recognize infinitives can be terribly helpful.

16. I desired to learn Russian.

17. I want to be a good student.

18. To be a man, I learned how to accept things.

19. To go to the open market is a thrill.

20. For studying, I like to rise early.

21. We thought about falling.

22. I took him there to register.

23. To cry is considered weak.

24. To get stronger, he started lifting weights every day.

25. You can't learn to drive in one day.

26. To fly takes coordination.

27. Stuttering can be helped.

28. To cure herself, the woman took antibiotics.

29. I think learning is important.

30. To eat until you are full is nonsense.

31. Stuffing yourself can't be healthy.

32. He asked me to use my car.

EXERCISE 7.12

33. He advised me to exercise more.

34. I, however, decided to ignore his advice.

35. A child learns to manipulate at a young age.

36. This is used for writing.

37. For racing, one needs nerves of steel.

38. Trying to deceive is not a very good idea.

39. Eating too much salt is dangerous.

40. Ordering your boss isn't smart.

41. He indicated he would never agree to give up.

EXERCISE 7.12

Exercise 7.13: Pronoun-Antecedent Agreement
Direction: *Fill in the blank with the appropriate pronoun.*

1. He left_____coat.
2. They left_____coats.
3. We left_____groceries.
4. The little boy ate_____apples.
5. Sally claims it is_____. (belongs to Sally)
6. We want_____grades. (the class's)
7. She ate_____tail. (of the animal)

Answer Key

Answers to Exercise 7.1

Directions: Punctuate the following sentences.

1. I did three things at the store: I ate a sample of fruit; I had an encounter with an old friend; finally, I ran into my boss.

2. If I ever go to bed after midnight, I usually wake up with a headache the next morning, but I didn't this morning.

3. She said that she was only looking for one thing at her new job: money!

4. Most likely, it will rain in the evening, and we will have to cancel our plans for the trip the next day.

5. I think, however, the day may turn out to be nice, because the weatherman said it will be sunny all weekend.

6. If I told you that I was a policeman, would you respect me differently?

7. I bought some milk, tea, a big container of flour, and some bread.

8. Although he really does not know his job, they will keep him on board until the summer is over.

9. The professor quoted several things in his lecture: first, the Civil War was an economic one; second, he indicated that the migration forced the South to take a different approach to its economics; and, most importantly, the outcome was a higher expanse of trade in the North.

10. Now, I know you are a little leery of meeting new people, but I want you to try and open up, because we love you.

11. If I were a woman, I think I would be just like me.

12. I don't want any candy, and he doesn't want any either.

13. I can't have any coffee, nor can I have tea after dinner.

14. He went to his mother's house; then, he went to the Jones' house.

15. He is, to put it lightly, a very rude person.

16. The man was, according to the police, a loner who had had a fight with the store's owner before closing time.

Answers to Exercise 7.2

Directions: Punctuate the following sentences. Make all answers only one sentence.

1. The girl, the sister, the mother, and the boyfriend all were injured in the plane accident, but, thank God, no one was killed.

2. Because he was my friend, I did not say anything; however, I will say something next time, because that behavior is totally unacceptable.

3. Since I was the fastest of the group, the coach made me run more, study harder material, and clean his car every week.

4. I left early, but, if I want to get there in time, I will have to hurry even more.

5. I talked with the man; then, I turned to the professor, but I'll never carry on, at least try not to, two conversations at once again.

6. I came early, so I could get a good seat.

7. When I was a kid, I used to fly a kite weekly.

8. I would've found the keys, but I got a call, and you know how my mother talks.

9. To win the game, they cheated every chance they got.

10. Today, I talked with Robbie, ate lunch at the restaurant, and went to a movie. But, believe me, I'm tired.

Answers to Exercise 7.3

Directions: Punctuate the following sentences. There may be several options. Correct all mistakes that you find.

1. I went to class and studied afterward; then, I went over to Tom's restaurant, and I met some of my classmates.

2. Slipping on the ice is never fun, but, unfortunately, it's a hazard of living in a cold part of the world; then again, I'd rather live here than in Africa.

3. Call me crazy, but I think that you should go to the man and apologize; after all, you were in the wrong just as much as him.

4. Do you think that you'll ever have your own apartment? I can't live like this anymore. You know that you're not the easiest person to get along with.

5. I certainly understand when a man loses his desire to go to work,

but, on the other hand, I could never buy into the idea of quitting life completely.

6. If I were you, I would try to fix my car before the cold weather set in.

7. She strolled along the riverbank and eyed the horizon, but, nevertheless, she was still lonely in that she had lost the one and only person she had ever trusted.

8. Stand straight. Now, raise your left arm.

9. If you, my one and only friend, were in trouble, I would do all I could, if possible, to fix everything, but only with you.

10. The chief of the department, who is also my friend, told me three things: the day was long, today is good, and he was tired.

11. Bluntly put, I couldn't have said it better myself, because I am a believer in justice, unlike you. However, you should never talk badly, at least around those of us who do believe.

12. He said, and I quote, "This is the best team I've ever seen."

13. According to the doctor, she could live, but *Digest* said, and this is a quote, "There is a 90 percent success rate in women 30 to 40 years of age."

14. Once, I was a young man, but I aged, as all before me have done.

15. If this world were mine, I would feed the hungry, shelter the homeless, and find a way to a better life (,); [see note] at least I would certainly try. (This can be considered an afterthought with only the comma after *life*, but the sentence should have a semicolon.)

16. To find a good bank takes tenacity, skill, and a lot of luck. One can quit, but he'll never get what he wants, so ask what you need to know.

17. Therefore, he was stranded; moreover, he had no money and no friends, and he was a long way from home.

18. I received many things, such as socks, pants, and shirts, but I like to be honest. The socks, the black ones, were the best.

19. I saw a good sport, namely kickboxing, but, when I saw a guy get killed, I stopped patronizing it altogether.

20. My friend plays rugby. The other plays nothing, and the other sleeps all day.

21. Walking along the road, he thought of life, liberty, and his happiness, until he was flattened by a gust of wind; then, he only thought about, according to him, catching his breath.

22. Running the track can be good; however, it is exhausting, especially on days when one is already tired, but I digress.

23. You know, John, I've always wanted to be the president of the U.S., but now I'm too old.

24. She did three things: she ate out; she studied; then, she retired.

Answers to Exercise 7.4

Directions: Choose the correct answer.

1. Could you tell me_____? (**a**)
   a. what kind of drink she prefers
   b. what kind of drink would she prefer
   c. what kind of drinking would she prefer
   d. what kind of drink does she prefer

2. If the boy had listened to me, _____. (**c**)
   a. he would had have taken the job
   b. he had have been taking the job
   c. he would have taken the job
   d. he would have been taken the job

3. She is _____. That is why I listen to her. (**c**)
   a. interest
   b. interested
   c. interesting
   d. interests

4. The land _____ is located in the forest. (**e**)
   a. that my father bought it
   b. which it my father bought
   c. which my father has bought it
   d. which has bought my father
   e. which my father bought

5. A birthday present _____ by my wife. (**c**)
   a. was to me given
   b. was me given
   c. was given to me
   d. was gaven me

6. _____ the manual, you must know English. (**d**)
   a. To reading

    b. To have been read by

    c. To be read

    d. To read

7. Do all of the employees at work understand _____? **(d)**

    a. why does the boss allow them to stay

    b. why does the boss allows them to stay

    c. why the boss he allows them to stay

    d. why the boss allows them to stay

8. The students have been waiting _____. **(d)**

    a. since two hours

    b. since two hours ago

    c. for two hours ago

    d. for two hours

9. Amy would like to get a car, and _____. **(d)**

    a. so do I

    b. so will I

    c. so I do, too

    d. so would I

10. I went to the store _____. **(b)**

    a. so to get a coke.

    b. so I could get a coke

    c. to be getting a coke

    d. so to be getting a coke

11. It is freezing out here now. You must_____cold. Do you want my coat? **(d)**

    a. get

    b. be get cold

    c. are getting

    d. be getting

12. I would buy a Mercedes if the price_____. But, it is. **(d)**

    a. wasn't so expensive

    b. isn't so expensive

    c. hadn't been so expensive

    d. weren't so expensive

13. John got Bob_____the car. **(c)**

    a. wash

b. washing

c. to wash

d. to washed

14. If it _____ so gloomy, it would have been nice weather. (**b**)

a. wasn't

b. hadn't been

c. weren't

d. isn't

15. _____ is broken, can you call me instead? (**b**)

a. So my clock

b. Because my clock

c. Since my clock it

d. So my clock it

16. The steak _____ was very tough. (**d**)

a. which we ordered it

b. that we ordered it

c. which one we ordered

d. which we ordered

17. We tried _____, but to no avail. (**d**)

a. to be having the car fixed

b. to have the car fixing

c. to had the car fixed

d. to have the car fixed

18. _____ is very annoying. (**b**)

a. To be interrupting by someone

b. Being interrupted by someone

c. To interrupt by someone

d. To have been interrupted by someone

19. Can you tell me _____? (**d**)

a. where was he sitting

b. where was he sit

c. where he was sit

d. where he was sitting

Answers to Exercise 7.5

Directions: Change the following sentences from active to passive voice.

1. The boys played football.

    Football was played by the boys.

2. The army was flying helicopters over the base late at night.

    Helicopters were being flown by the army over the base late at night.

3. The girls achieved the highest award given by the organization.

    The highest award given by the organization was achieved by the girls.

4. The baseball team won most of the games they played this year.

    Most of the games they played this year were won by the baseball team.

5. The jury decided the fate of the accused murderers.

    The fate of the accused murderers was decided by the jury.

6. The plane crashed in the Andes late last night.

    The plane was crashed in the Andes late last night.

7. No one survived the crash in the Andes last night.

    The crash in the Andes last night was not survived by anyone.

8. The group of boys taunted the girls walking across the yard.

    The girls walking across the yard were taunted by the group of boys.

9. The kittens roamed about the yard playing.

    The yard was roamed about by the kittens playing.

10. The professor pounded the desk in frustration.

    The desk was pounded in frustration by the professor.

11. The teacher modeled his class after what he was taught.

    The class was modeled by the teacher after what he was taught.

12. The bear splashed through the stream clumsily.

    The stream was clumsily splashed through by the bear.

13. The best student flunked the exam.

    The exam was flunked by the best student.

14. The girl perused the headlines for any word of snow.

    The headlines were perused by the girl for any word of snow.

15. The fat, old, ugly bear consumed the picnic.

    The picnic was consumed by the fat, old, ugly bear.

16. Beside the road, a snake swallowed the mouse.

> The mouse was swallowed by a snake beside the road.

17. The regiment formed a battle line.

> A battle line was formed by the regiment.

18. The ball hit the backboard and made a noise.

> The blackboard was hit and a noise was made by the ball.

19. The policemen captured the murderer behind the station.

> The murderer was captured behind the station by the policemen.

20. An old lady hobbled along the sidewalk.

> The sidewalk was hobbled along by the old lady.

21. A dog ripped open the sack when he smelled the meat.

> The sack was ripped open by a dog when he smelled the meat.

Answers to Exercise 7.6

Directions: Change from active to passive voice.

1. No change

2. A wolf was encountered by us along the highway.

3. The heart is helped by singing a song. (*by* + gerund)

4. A merriment in the heart is achieved by singing.

5. Ill will was distributed around his neighborhood by the old miser.

6. No change

7. The car was made to shine by the glisten of the lights.

8. The brakes were made to squeak loudly as he applied them.

9. The den was pranced through by the cub.

10. A trickling sound was made by the water as it ran down the drain.

11. No change: Can make gerund. Cheating was done by the goalie . . .

12. The copier was repaired by him.

13. Dinner is being eaten later now.

14. The ashtray was tossed into the receptacle by the lady.

15. No change: Can make gerund. Whirring was made by the computer . . .

Answers to Exercise 7.7

Directions: Change the following sentence from active to passive, and punctuate it.

The man wrapped the gift then he hid the bottle in the fireplace next the man threw out the extra paper finally he discarded the evidence

The gift was wrapped by the man; then, the bottle was hidden by him in the fireplace. Next, the extra paper was thrown out by the man. Finally, the evidence was discarded by him.

Answers to Exercise 7.8

Directions: Find the independent clause and the dependent clause in each sentence. Mark the independent clause by underlining it, and write *IC.* Indicate the dependent clause by writing *DC.* Do not rely on ellipsis to make a clause.

Legend: IC is underlined; DC is italicized.

IC   DC
1. The man became extremely irritated *when the little boy begged for candy.*

DC   IC
2. Once, *when I was just a small boy about five,* my dad took me to the zoo.

   IC   IC   IC
3. I hate to eat and run, but I must inform you now, so you won't get angry later.

IC   DC   IC   DC
4. The man *whom I always called my uncle* was the guy *whom they called Dewey.*

   DC   IC (S = DC)
5. *As he learned later on in life,* the things that come easy are not always the best things to have.

IC   (DC)

6. <u>I think</u> ***that running*** <u>on an empty stomach is a bad idea</u>.

IC   DC   IC

7. <u>The fat cat</u>, ***the one I caught eating out of the trash,*** <u>was run over</u>.

IC   DC (DO)

8. <u>The strange culture teaches a young man</u> ***that he must adapt.***

IC

9. <u>Eating after midnight must be terrible for the system</u>.

IC   DC (DO)

10. <u>Do you know</u> ***if today is cold?***

Answers to Exercise 7.9

Directions: Identify the complete subject by underlining it.

1. <u>The old man down the street</u> makes me very angry sometimes.
2. <u>The little girl to whom you gave some candy </u>is a good student.
3. <u>The old, rickety truck</u> blew up on the highway.
4. <u>The stately living in homes lose</u> their dignity if not treated wisely.
5. <u>To lose at what you love the most</u> crushes one after too many losses.
6. <u>Running on a full tank of premium</u> lessens the wear on an engine.
7. <u>The administering of unlawful drugs without permission</u> is a felony.
8. <u>To slowly and painfully wither away</u> is a fact of life.
9. <u>Eating from the fruit of life</u> sustains the health.
10. <u>Evangelism in the West</u> is on the rise.
11. <u>"To rise with the chickens"</u> is an old phrase.
12. <u>I</u> love my family.

Answers to Exercise 7.10

Directions: Identify the subject complement by underlining it.

1. He looks <u>tired</u>.
2. It seems <u>awfully cold</u> today.
3. The look in her eye was <u>mesmerizing</u>.
4. To doubt oneself is <u>the ultimate insult</u>.
5. Thinking of you only makes <u>me free</u>.
6. Arbitrarily making judgments is <u>not a shrewd business practice</u>.
7. I have over the course of time become <u>a man</u>.
8. He appears to be <u>the steadiest person I know</u>.
9. A catastrophic event seems to be <u>almost life-sustaining</u>.
10. To think that I almost lost is <u>unthinkable</u>.
11. Mission Control is <u>one of the largest and most comprehensive centers</u>.
12. Walking alone late at night is <u>certainly a chilling experience</u>.
13. The order which came from above looked like <u>a forged document</u>.
14. Being tall and having a good wife and beautiful children is <u>great</u>.
15. To necessitate the arrival of reinforcements equals <u>trouble</u>.
16. "They call me trouble," is <u>what he said</u>.
17. My favorite pastime is <u>probably going to the lake at sundown</u>.
18. What he says and what he does are <u>two totally separate things</u>.
19. Finding all of these stupid, inane grammatical points is <u>frustrating</u>.
20. Walking for exercise became <u>the one most tolerable exercise</u>.

Answers to Exercise 7.11

Directions: Identify the direct object with *DO* and the indirect object with *IO*.

Legend = Complete DO is underlined and IO is italicized.

1. I learned <u>that we had issued *__him__*</u> a book.
2. After receiving the answer, I passed it to ***the dean.***
3. To give <u>the book</u> to ***them*** was a mistake.
4. I think <u>you must learn to give your time more freely</u>.
5. Understand <u>the lesson</u>, and you will succeed.
6. I had him administer <u>the exam</u>.
7. If you write <u>the letter</u>, I will take <u>the money</u>.

8. Did you tell **him** to sit down?

9. I learned the method in a short time.

10. Eat more fruit, and you will not be tired.

11. Can you say anything?

12. I did not think so.

13. If I say no, will you leave?

14. Write all the answers.

15. Where did you place the file?

16. I eat fish frequently, but I only told **him** the story yesterday.

17. Read the article to understand the meaning.

18. Pop that top, and we will celebrate.

19. I hate to wait.

20. He wants to leave.

21. I have a desire for tacos.

Answers to Exercise 7.12

Directions: Gerunds and infinitives have three functions: (1) to act as the subject, (2) to act as the direct object, and (3) to indicate reason. Indicate *I* for infinitive and *1, 2,* or *3* for function, and *G* for gerund and *1, 2,* or *3* for function.

   G3

1. I am here for learning.

   I3   I3

2. To learn, we must be prepared to study.

   I3   I2

3. To regain the love of his life, the man learned to write poetry.

      G3 (2 = obj of prep) I (1 = SC)

4. The purpose of writing is to communicate.

     I3

5. I have been waiting to speak with you.

     I3

6. In order to revive him, she administered mouth-to-mouth resuscitation.

     I3

7. She was afraid to go out at dawn.

     I2

8. I want <u>to leave</u> at noon.

    G2

9. I heard <u>whispering</u> over the phone.

    G1

10. <u>Walking</u> on ice can be dangerous.

    I2

11. I am learning <u>to tread</u> water.

    I1

12. <u>To think</u> of her made him crazy.

    G1

13. <u>Reading</u> is not the easiest thing sometimes.

  I2   I3

14. If you are wanting <u>to ride,</u> meet me at 6:00 <u>to go</u> over there.

  G1 I1 or 2

15. <u>Learning to recognize</u> infinitives can be terribly helpful.

    I2

16. I desired <u>to learn</u> Russian.

    I2

17. I want <u>to be</u> a good student.

        I3

18. <u>To be</u> a man, I learned how to <u>accept</u> things.

    I1

19. <u>To go</u> to the open market is a thrill.

    G3   I2

20. <u>For studying</u>, I like <u>to rise</u> early.

    G2

21. We thought <u>about falling</u>.

    I3

22. I took him there <u>to register</u>.

    I1

23. <u>To cry</u> is considered weak.

    I3

24. <u>To get</u> stronger, he started lifting weights every day.

    I2

25. You can't learn <u>to drive</u> in one day.

I1

26. <u>To fly</u> takes coordination.

G1

27. <u>Stuttering</u> can be helped.

I3

28. <u>To cure</u> herself, the woman took antibiotics.

G1 & G2

29. I think <u>learning</u> is important.

I1

30. <u>To eat</u> until you are full is nonsense.

G1

31. <u>Stuffing</u> yourself can't be healthy.

I2

32. He asked me <u>to use</u> my car.

I2

33. He advised me <u>to exercise</u> more.

I2

34. I, however, decided <u>to ignore</u> his advice.

I2

35. A child learns <u>to manipulate</u> at a young age.

G3

36. This is used <u>for writing</u>.

G3

37. <u>For racing,</u> one needs nerves of steel.

G1   I2 or 1

38. <u>Trying to deceive</u> is not a very good idea.

G1

39. <u>Eating</u> too much salt is dangerous.

G1

40. <u>Ordering</u> your boss isn't smart.

I2

41. He indicated he would never agree <u>to give up.</u>

Answers to Exercise 7.13:
Pronoun-Antecedent Agreement

He left his coat.

They left their coats.

We left our groceries.

The little boy ate his apples.

The girl claims it is hers.

I want our grades

She ate its tail.

More Exercises

EXERCISE 7.14

Exercise 7.14: Adjectivals

Directions: *Underline the adjective or the phrase or clause acting like an adjective.*

1. He gave up the whole idea, by far the smartest thing he ever did.
2. How he knew is the most baffling.
3. The unusual things faded away.
4. The wooden house burned to the ground.
5. The enlightened despot abdicated the throne.
6. In a fit of rage, the man blew up.
7. I could not understand how such a meager sum panned out.
8. If I had completely understood, I would have written the blackest of comedies.
9. I had completely denied the reprehensible truth.
10. Knowing the obvious is helpful.
11. I shuffled along the less-traveled highways.
12. The repressive mandate was stricken.
13. I would acknowledge the weakest of all before anything.
14. If I saw a horrible event like that, I'd leave.
15. To be like that, I would consult the most expert advice.
16. I see the ugliest answer coming out.

EXERCISE 7.14

17. I want the complete truth.
18. The fledgling bird fell from the nest.
19. The running train is arriving on time.
20. The boiled water is more sanitary.
21. The man whom you saw is my friend.
22. The girl pointed at the man, whoever it was.
23. I saw the one that you saw.
24. Ask me, the one who knows, tomorrow.
25. Most despicable, he stole the candy from the baby.

Answers to Exercise 7.14: Adjectivals

Directions: Underline the adjective or the phrase or clause acting like an adjective.

1. He gave up the <u>whole</u> idea, by far <u>the smartest thing he ever did</u>.
2. How he knew is the <u>most baffling</u>.
3. The <u>unusual</u> things faded away.
4. The <u>wooden</u> house burned to the ground.
5. The <u>enlightened</u> despot abdicated the throne.
6. In a fit <u>of rage</u>, the man blew up.
7. I could not understand how such a <u>meager</u> sum panned out.
8. If I had completely understood, I would have written the <u>blackest</u> of comedies.
9. I had completely denied the <u>reprehensible</u> truth.
10. Knowing the <u>very</u> obvious is helpful.
11. I shuffled along the <u>less-traveled</u> highways.
12. The <u>repressive</u> mandate was stricken.
13. I would acknowledge <u>the weakest of all</u> before anything.
14. If I saw a <u>horrible</u> event like that, I'd leave.
15. To be like that, I would consult the most <u>expert</u> advice.
16. I see the <u>ugliest</u> answer coming out.
17. I want the <u>complete</u> truth.
18. The <u>fledgling</u> bird fell from the nest.
19. The <u>running</u> train is arriving on time.
20. The <u>boiled</u> water is more <u>sanitary</u>.
21. The man <u>whom you saw</u> is my friend.

22. The girl pointed out the man, <u>whoever it was</u>.
23. I saw the one <u>that you saw</u>.
24. Ask me, <u>the one who knows</u>, tomorrow.
25. Most <u>despicable</u>, he stole the candy from the baby.

Exercise 7.15: Adjectives and Adverbs

Directions: *Circle the correct answer.*

1. I will be running the (fast, faster, fastest).
2. The girl was acting in the most (vile, viler, vilest) of fashions.
3. The little steamboat moved along (swimming, swimmingly, swimminglier).
4. The captain berated his men (consistent, constant, consistently, constantively).
5. He reacted in a more (violently, violent, violenter) fashion than usual.
6. (Suppressing, suppressingly, suppressive) his anger, he quietly acquiesced.
7. (Unawares of, unweary of, unaware of) the danger, the officer proceeded into the abandoned building.
8. He wrote to me (haphazard, haphazardly, haphazardish) until the day he died.
9. If the man fell for the scam (unsuspectedly, unsuspicingly, unsuspectivedly, unsuspecting), he gave her all of the money.
10. The ironic thing is the (sheepish, sheepishly, sheepishingly) grin he carried around.
11. The troop's advance was (slowly, slowingly, slow) due to the rain.
12. After the rain, the mudslide (gradual, gradually, more gradual) gathered momentum.
13. The onset was (slow, slowly, slowishly) at first; then, it picked up speed at an (alarming, alarmed, alarmingly) fast pace.
14. The character was dark, and barked orders in a (quite, quiet, quietly) manner.

EXERCISE 7.15

15. She sat in (unproductively, unproducive, unproductive) form.
16. All the while (belittling, belittled, belittledly) them, he ranted and raved at his employees.
17. (Floundered, floundering, flounderingly) about by the waves, the sailor could hardly keep his head above water.
18. The opponent gave in (willing, willingly, willishly).

Answers to Exercise 7.15: Adjectives and Adverbs

Directions: Circle the correct answer.

1. I will be running the (fast, faster, **fastest**).
2. The girl was acting in the most (**vile,** viler, vilest) of fashions.
3. The little steamboat moved along (swimming, **swimmingly**, swimminglier).
4. The captain berated his men (consistent, constant, **constantively**).
5. He reacted in a more (violently, **violent,** violenter) fashion than usual.
6. (**Suppressing,** suppressingly, suppressive) his anger, he quietly acquiesced.
7. (Unawares of, unweary of, **unaware of**) the danger, the officer proceeded into the abandoned building.
8. He wrote to me (haphazard, **haphazardly**, haphazardish) until the day he died.
9. If the man fell for the scam (unsuspectedly, **unsuspectingly,** unsuspectivedly, unsuspecting), he gave her all of the money.
10. The ironic thing is the (**sheepish,** sheepishly, sheepishingly) grin he carried around.
11. The troop's advance was (slowly, slowingly, **slow**) due to the rain.
12. After the rain, the mudslide (gradual, **gradually,** more gradual) gathered momentum.
13. The onset was (**slow,** slowly, slowishly) at first; then, it picked up speed at an (alarming, alarmed, **alarmingly**) fast pace.
14. The character was dark, and barked orders in a (quite, **quiet,** quietly) manner.
15. She sat in (unproductively, unproducive, **unproductive**) form.

16. All the while (**belittling**, belittled, belittledly) them, he ranted and raved at his employees.

17. (**Floundered,** floundering, flounderingly) about by the waves, the sailor could hardly keep his head above water.

18. The opponent gave in (willing, **willingly,** willishly).

Exercise 7.16: Reflexive Pronouns

Directions: *Circle the correct answer.*

1. The boy burned (hisself, his self, himself, him self).

2. The ticket agent fixed the arrangements (hisself, himself, themselves, themselves).

3. The team were congratulatory among (itself, themselves, theirself, themself).

4. She saw them looking at (theirselves, themselves, theirself, them selves).

5. The coach told the team to take a look at (itself, themselves, themselves, they selves).

6. The snake was supposed to have been able to bite (itself, theirselves, themself, oneself).

7. The debating of (oneself, itself, theirself, themselves) in public will make observers think one is crazy.

8. Access to the bank is limited only to patrons (theirself, himself, itself, themselves).

9. The owners (theirselves, themselves, them self, them selves) were angry.

10. I scolded them and suggested they watch (theirselves, themselves, they selves, them selves) in the future.

11. The dogs started to turn on (one other, each one, one another, each there other).

12. The movie caused each one of us to look at (our self, ourself, ourselves, himself).

13. I told the soldier to wash (his self, himself, him self, his selves).

EXERCISE 7.16

14. The dog wagged the tail (him self, his self, itself, him self).
15. The snake curled (itself, her self, himself, themselves).
16. The man indicated that he (his self, himself, itself, by hisself) would do the taxes.
17. If he had mailed the letter (hisself, himself, they selves, themselves), he would not be so angry.
18. I told (me self, my self, myself, himself) that it would be all right.
19. I always have to remind (me self, me, my self, myself) that it is early.
20. The officer reminded the boys to strap (theirselves, themselves, itself, theirself) in.

Answers to Exercise 7.16: Reflexive Pronouns
Directions: Circle the correct answer.

1. The boy burned (hisself, his self, **himself,** him self).
2. The ticket agent fixed the arrangements (hisself, **himself,** themselves, themselves).
3. The team members were congratulatory among (itself, **themselves,** theirself, themself).
4. She saw them looking at (theirselves, **themselves,** theirself, them selves).
5. The coach told the team to take a look at (**itself,** themselves, themselves, they selves).
6. The snake was supposed to have been able to eat (**itself,** theirselves, themself, oneself).
7. The debating of (**oneself,** itself, theirself, themselves) in public will make observers think one is crazy.
8. Access to the bank is limited only to patrons (theirself, himself, itself, **themselves**).
9. The owners (theirselves, **themselves,** them self, them selves) were angry.
10. I scolded them and suggested they watch (theirselves, **themselves,** they selves, them selves) in the future.
11. The dogs started to turn on (one other, each one, **one another,** each there other).

12. The movie caused each one of us to look at (our self, ourself, **ourselves,** himself).

13. I told the soldier to wash (his self, **himself,** him self, his selves).

14. The dog (him self, his self, **itself,** him self) wagged the tail.

15. The snake curled (**itself,** her self, himself, themselves).

16. The man indicated that he (his self, **himself,** itself, by hisself) would do the taxes.

17. If he had mailed the letter (hisself, **himself,** they selves, themselves), he would not be so angry.

18. I told (me self, my self, **myself,** himself) that it would be all right.

19. I always have to remind (me self, me, my self, **myself**) that it is early.

20. The officer reminded the boys to strap (theirselves, **themselves,** itself, theirself) in.

Exercise 7.17 Pronouns: Subject/Object Cases

Directions: *Circle the best answer.*

1. The man asked the boys if (they, them, he, him) had brought the tools.

2. The boys said that (he, they, we, them) had not brought the tools.

3. If the senator was informed, the committee probably contacted (them, he, him, them) on the first meeting.

4. I could not say if the report was accurate in (its, it's, their, his) facts.

5. I asked (whom, who, they, we) would want cake.

6. He asked if I knew (who, whom, which, that) might have taken the truck.

7. I knew (who, whom) had taken it.

8. He had said (he, them, we, us, they) were investigating why the house was torched.

9. The whales had beached (herself, themself, themselves, itselves).

10. The little boy was informed by his father that the lawn would not mow (itself, their selves, it's self).

EXERCISE 7.17

11. The waiters had a meeting with the waitresses to ensure (them selves, theirselves, themselves, those selves) of jobs.
12. The cell began to feed on (itself, its' selves, their self, they) for nourishment.
13. I know where (one, ones, them, ourselves) goes by the river.
14. The red ants broke up and began fighting (their selves, themselves, itself, its self).
15. The team lost respect for (itself, themselves, there selves, theirselves) after it intentionally lost the game.

Answers to Exercise 7.17 Pronouns: Subject/Object Cases

Directions: Circle the best answer.

1. The man asked the boys if (**they,** them, he, him) had brought the tools.
2. The boys said that (he, **they,** we, them) had not brought the tools.
3. If the senator was informed, the committee probably contacted (them, he, **him,** them) on the first meeting.
4. I could not say if the report was accurate in (**its,** it's, their his) facts.
5. I asked (whom, **who**, they, we) would want cake.
6. He asked if I knew (**who,** whom, which, that) might have taken the truck.
7. I knew (**who,** whom) had taken it.
8. He had said (he, them, we, us, **they**) were investigating why the house was torched.
9. The whales had beached (herself, themself, **themselves**, itselves).
10. The little boy was informed by his father that the lawn would not mow (**itself,** their selves, it's self).
11. The waiters had a meeting with the waitresses to ensure (them selves, theirselves, **themselves,** those selves) of jobs.
12. The cell began to feed on (**itself,** its' selves, their self, they) for nourishment.
13. I know where (**one,** ones, them, ourselves) goes by the river.

14. The red ants broke up and began fighting (their selves, **themselves,** itself, its self).

15. The team lost respect for (**itself,** themselves, them selves, theirselves) after it intentionally lost the game.

EXERCISE 7.18

Exercise 7.18: Possessive Pronouns
Directions: *Circle the correct answer.*

1. The air is not (ours, her's, theres, our).
2. The desk that was (mine, my, ours) is now at my mother's house.
3. To be (ones', oneself, one's own, onesown) man requires hard work.
4. The cat wagged (its, their, its') tail.
5. The boys made sure (they're, there, theirs, their) party was loud.
6. Poverty caused (their, there, it's, its) share of problems when the economy suffered problems.
7. I do not see (who's, which, whose, whos') car it was, but the owner was not driving.
8. (Whoever, whatever, whomever) he said was certainly convincing.
9. The man, (whoever, whomever, however, forever) he is, pulled the people to safety.
10. The story seemed to delight all the people, giving to (each, one, every, own) a sense of belonging and worth.
11. (Somebodies, somebody's, anybody's, anybodies) towel was swept away by the current.
12. The (companies's, company's, companies', companys') staff ignored safety regulations.
13. The (boy's, boys') dog was only used to one owner.
14. The (Galapagos', Galapagos's) territory is more extensive than one may think.
15. The (minds', mind's, minds's) eye shoots forth in dreams, according to the book.
16. Doesn't (anybodys', anybody's, anybodies, anybodies') watch work?

EXERCISE 7.18

17. He looked at (everyones, everyones', everyone's, every one's) pockets before he exited the store.
18. The (childrens', childrens, children's) posters hung on the wall.
19. I verified the (atlas', atlas's, atlases', atlases') facts.
20. The (Jones's Joneses, Jones'es, Jones') family car stopped.
21. The concurrent use of the two (cabin's, cabins', cabins'es, cabins) shared plumbing erupted in problems.

Answers to Exercise 7.18: Possessive Pronouns

Directions: Circle the correct answer.

1. The air is not (**ours,** her's, theres, our).
2. The desk that was (**mine,** my, ours) is now at my mother's house.
3. To be (ones', oneself, **one's own,** onesown) man requires hard work.
4. The cat wagged (**its,** their, its') tail.
5. The boys made sure (they're, there, theirs, **their**) party was loud.
6. Poverty caused (their, there, it's, **its**) share of problems when the economy suffered problems.
7. I do not see (who's, which, **whose,** whos') car it was, but the owner was not driving.
8. (Whoever, **whatever,** whomever) he said was certainly convincing.
9. The man, (**whoever,** whomever, however, forever) he is, pulled the people to safety.
10. The story seemed to delight all the people, giving to (**each,** one, every, own) a sense of belonging and worth.
11. (Somebodies, **somebody's,** anybody's, anybodies) towel was swept away by the current.
12. The (companies's, **company's,** companies', companys') staff ignored safety regulations.
13. The (**boy's,** boys') dog was only used to one owner.
14. The (Galapagos', **Galapagos's**) territory is more extensive than one may think.
15. The (minds', **mind's,** minds's) eye shoots forth in dreams, according to the book.
16. Doesn't (anybodys', **anybody's,** anybodies, anybodies') watch work?

17. He looked at (everyones, everyones', **everyone's**, every one's) pockets before he exited the store.

18. The (childrens', childrens, **children's**) posters hung on the wall.

19. I verified the (atlas', **atlas's,** atlases', atlases') facts.

20. The (**Jones's** Joneses, Jones'es, Jones') family car stopped.

21. The concurrent use of the two (cabin's, **cabins',** cabins'es, cabins) shared plumbing erupted in problems.

Exercise 7.19: Possessives

Directions: *Circle the correct answer.*

1. The (mens', men's, man's mans') bathroom is across the hall.

2. The (girls', girl's, girls's, girlses') bathroom is downstairs.

3. If the (childs's, childs', childrens', children's) balloon flew away, I'd see it.

4. The (dogs, dog's, dogs') house got wet, so I let her sleep inside.

5. The (play's, plays, plays') actors were applauded on closing night.

6. The (rats', rat's, rats's) tails began to fall off due to the experimental medicine.

7. Many (peoples', people's, peoples's) houses were blown away during the storm.

8. The (womens, womans', women' women's) auxiliary club meets tonight.

9. The (mices', mice's, mouses', mouse') hole was plugged up.

10. A (waiters', waiters's, waiter's) job is hard.

11. The (waitresses', waitress's, waitress') tips were not enough to satisfy her requirement.

12. We are tired of (each's other, each others', each other's) bad habits.

13. The blouse is (her's, hers', hers).

14. This is (your's, yours, yours').

15. The (crisis', crises's, crisis's) impact tore the land apart.

16. The (teams', team's, teams's) requests for all of those in that league were boiled down to one item: they should be allowed to be free agents.

17. He said he wanted (ten dollars', ten dollar's, ten dollars's) worth of gas.
18. I went to (Bob and Jane's, Bob's and Jane's, Bob's and Jane) wedding.
19. It is (mine's, mines, mine, mines').
20. The boat is (our's, ours', ours).

Answers to Exercise 7.19: Possessives

Directions: Circle the correct answer.

1. The (mens', **men's,** man's mans') bathroom is across the hall. The possessive of the plural is always *men's* unless one uses *man* to refer to mankind in general. For example, the sentence *Man's accomplishments in space travel are astounding* categorizes man and men collectively as one species, thereby allowing the unit to be made possessive by *'s*, with the plural suggested. With *men*, in that the plural is formed through gradation (changing only the inside vowel), one makes the plural possessive by *'s*; this is true with *women's, children's, gentlemen's, sheep's, geese's, feet's,* and *teeth's,* as well.

2. The (**girls',** girl's, girls's, girlses') bathroom is downstairs. The bathroom is open to all of the girls.

3. If the (childs's, childs', childrens', **children's**) balloon flew away, I'd see it. See number 1.

4. The (dogs, **dog's,** dogs') house got wet, so I let her sleep inside.

5. The (**play's,** plays, plays') actors were applauded on closing night.

6. The (**rats',** rat's, rats's) tails began to fall off due to the experimental medicine.

7. Many (peoples', **people's,** peoples's) houses were blown away during the storm. See number 1.

8. The (womens, womans', women', **women's**) auxiliary club meets tonight.

9. The (mices', **mice's,** mouses', mouse') hole was plugged up. *Mice* follows the rule described in number 1.

10. A (waiters', waiters's, **waiter's**) job is hard.

11. The (waitresses', **waitress's,** waitress') tips were not enough to satisfy her requirement. *Waitress* is singular; therefore, we simply add *'s.*

12. We are tired of (each's other, each others', **each other's**) bad habits.

13. The blouse is (her's, hers', **hers**).

> **GRAMMAR NOTE:** Hers, yours, *and* ours *never take an apostrophe or an object.*

14. This is (your's, **yours,** yours').

15. The (crisis', crises's, **crisis's**) impact tore the land apart. *Crisis's* is singular possessive. One crisis, two crises = one crisis's impact, two crises' impact.

16. The (**teams',** team's, teams's) requests for all of those in that league were boiled down to one item: they should be allowed to be free agents. *Those* and *they* indicate that *teams'* is plural possessive.

17. He said he wanted (**ten dollars',** ten dollar's, ten dollars's) worth of gas. The worth is equal to ten dollars; therefore, the possessive is plural.

18. I went to (**Bob and Jane's, Bob's and Jane's,** Bob's and Jane) wedding. Both underlined answers are correct, yet *Bob and Jane* is one phrase, and attaching the *'s* at the end is easier.

19. It is (mine's, mines, **mine,** mines'). See number 1.

20. The boat is (our's, ours', **ours**).

EXERCISE 7.20

Exercise 7.20: *For, Since, Ago*

Directions: *Make answers using the following cues.*
You may need to change the positioning of the cue phrase or rewrite.

1. How long have you been here?
   _____one hour.

2. When did you arrive?
   _____one hour.

3. How long have you been exercising?
   _____8:00.

4. When did he call you?
   _____one day.

5. When did you hear about the test?
   _____two weeks ago.

6. How long have you spoken Spanish?
   _____twenty years.

7. How long will you stay here?
   _____a month.

8. How long have you known Jill?
   _____one year.

9. How long will you be studying?
   _____as long as it takes to learn.

10. How long will you be at the store?
    _____a minute.

11. When did you start coming to this lake?
    _____I was a child.

12. How long have you been swimming without a vest?
    _____as long as I can remember.

13. By next Tuesday, how long will you have been here?
    _____at least a week.

14. When did you see your father?
    _____in May.

15. How long were you in Europe?
    _____almost a month.

EXERCISE 7.20

16. How long have you been smoking?

_____a year.

17. When were you watching the game?

_____about half the morning.

18. How long has it been since you smoked?

_____over a year.

19. How long will you be attending the meeting in London?

_____about a week.

20. How long will your stopover be in Russia?

_____at all.

Answers to Exercise 7.20: For, Since, Ago

Directions: Make answers using the following cues.

Answers may vary.

1. How long have you been here?

___I have been here for one hour.

2. When did you arrive?

___I arrived one hour ago.

3. How long have you been exercising?

___I have been exercising since 8:00.

4. When did he call you?

___He called me one day ago.

5. When did you hear about the test?

___I heard about the test two weeks ago.

6. How long have you spoken Spanish?

___I have been speaking Spanish for twenty years.

7. How long will you stay here?

___I will stay here for a month.

8. How long have you known Jill?

___I have known Jill for one year.

9. How long will you be studying?

___I will be studying for as long as it takes to learn.

___I will study for as long as it takes to learn.

10. How long will you be at the store?

___I will be at the store for a minute.

11. When did you start coming to this lake?

___I started coming to this lake when I was a child. Do not use *since*.

12. How long have you been swimming without a vest?

___I have been swimming without a vest for as long as I can remember.

13. By next Tuesday, how long will you have been here?

___By next Tuesday, I will have been here for at least a week.

14. When did you see your father?

___I saw my father in May.

15. How long were you in Europe?

___I was in Europe for almost a month.

16. How long have you been smoking?

___I have not smoked in a year. Must be a negative answer with *in a year*.

Or, I have not smoked for a year. (Negative or positive answer.)

17. When were you watching the game?

___I was watching the game about half the morning.

18. How long has it been since you smoked?

___I have not smoked in/for over a year.

19. How long will you be attending the meeting in London?

___I will be attending the meeting for about a week.

20. How long will your stopover be in Russia?

___I will not stop in Russia at all. Answer must be negative with *at all*.

Exercise 7.21: Conjunctions

Directions: *Choose the best answer: but, because, or, yet, for, and, neither/nor, so, either/or.*

1. She likes the light color,_____I like the dark one.
2. I wear the white one, _____it is cooler than the black one.
3. He is very irritating, _____I would like to work with him, because he is funny.
4. She does not like tea, _____ do I.
5. _____ you do it, _____ I will.
6. She did not want the bottle, _____ I didn't make her take it.
7. I would not have chosen him, _____ I do not trust him.
8. _____she lied, she was placed under arrest for perjury.
9. Bob, Ted, _____ Alice had cokes before dinner.
10. Bob and Ted, _____ not Alice, had cokes before dinner.
11. The candidate _____ denied the claim _____ confirmed it; therefore, we have no information from him.
12. The man will _____ go home _____ die trying, but he is certain-ly not staying here.
13. She gave him an ultimatum: _____ come home now, _____ stay away.

Answers to Exercise 7.21: Conjunctions

Directions: Choose the best answer: *but, because, or, yet, for, and, neither/nor, so, either/or.*

1. She likes the light color, <u>but</u> I like the dark one.
2. I wear the white one, <u>because</u> it is cooler than the black one.
3. He is very irritating, <u>but</u> I would like to work with him, because he is funny.
4. She does not like tea, <u>nor</u> do I.
5. <u>Either</u> you do it, <u>or</u> I will.
6. She did not want the bottle, <u>so</u> I didn't make her take it.
7. I would not have chosen him, <u>because</u> I do not trust him.
8. <u>Because</u> she lied, she was placed under arrest for perjury.
9. Bob, Ted, <u>and</u> Alice had cokes before dinner.

10. Bob and Ted, <u>but</u> not Alice, had cokes before dinner.

11. The candidate <u>neither</u> denied the claim <u>nor</u> confirmed it; therefore, we have no information from him.

12. The man will <u>either</u> go home <u>or</u> die trying, but he is certainly not staying here.

13. She gave him an ultimatum: <u>Either</u> come home now, <u>or</u> stay away.

Exercise 7.22: Parallelism

Directions: *Rewrite any part of the sentences below that may not be parallel.*

1. We ate early, ran the course, and went shopping.

2. I wished I had powers, he had the flu, and we all were having the ability to fly.

3. I organized the meeting, was basting the roast, and cleaned the house.

4. The men who were late were accused of misconduct, sent to jail, and were being fined for a huge sum.

5. If the dog had had enough to eat, it would not have returned later to be begging.

6. The most attractive elements of the film were its ability to enrapture the viewer, its overpowering ability to gladden those who could identify with the characters, and its ability to be enthralling, as well.

7. If you have gone to the store over there before, you would know how slow they are.

8. The best, the worst, and the medium are all welcome here.

9. I think only the hard-bitten could rely on, look forward to, and even insist that keeping the one thing the law had excluded.

10. If we had seen, had prevented the events beforehand, or have even thought about it, we would have done something to avoid the whole situation.

11. The worst snake of the bunch slithered its way into the underbrush, twisting its way around the back of the pole, and attacked.

12. The deranged psychotic yelled his demands to the guard, who, in turn, relayed them to the warden, who, in turn, was calling them into the police station.

13. The fat, old cat purred loudly, rubbed up against my leg, and waddling down the sidewalk.

14. The missile shot straight up, hovered at about 1,000 feet, and then had fallen.

15. The secretary looked up the word, muttered quietly, and was beginning typing.

Answers to Exercise 7.22: Parallelism

Directions: Rewrite any part of the sentences below that may not be parallel.

1. We ate early, ran the course, and **shopped.**

2. I wished I had powers, he had the flu, and we all **had** the ability to fly.

3. I organized the meeting, **basted** the roast, and cleaned the house.

4. The men who were late were accused of misconduct, sent to jail, and **fined** for a huge sum.

5. If the dog had had enough to eat, it would not have returned later **to beg.**

6. The most attractive elements of the film were its ability to enrapture the viewer, its overpowering ability to gladden those who could identify with the characters, and its ability **to enthrall,** as well.

7. If you **had gone** to the store over there before, you would know how slow they are.

8. The best, the worst, and the **mediocre** are all welcome here.

9. I think only the hard-bitten could rely **on,** look forward to, and even insist on keeping the one thing the law had excluded.

10. If we had seen, had prevented the events beforehand, or **had** even thought about it, we would have done something to avoid the whole situation.

11. The worst snake of the bunch slithered its way into the underbrush, **twisted** its way around the back of the pole, and attacked.

12. The deranged psychotic yelled his demands to the guard, who, in turn, relayed them to the warden, who, in turn, **called** them into the police station.

13. The fat, old cat purred loudly, rubbed up against my leg, and **wad-dled** down the sidewalk.

14. The missile shot straight up, hovered at about 1,000 feet, and then **fell.**

15. The secretary looked up the word, muttered quietly, and **began** typing (or, . . . *and typed*).

EXERCISE 7.23

Exercise 7.23: Faulty and Incomplete Comparisons

Directions: *Correct the sentences if there's a problem, or write C if correct.*

1. I hit the balls faster than John.

2. The train is slower than the car.

3. The trip to London is longer than New York.

4. I would have bought the green one, because it is more shorter than the red one.

5. They were all running fast, but Tom was the faster.

6. Swimming in the lake is better than the marina.

7. Running a long time is more detrimental to the shins than lifting weights.

8. I saw and liked the simpler one the more than the other type.

9. The outside was cold, but the inside was colder, also.

10. I run better than Mary.

11. She is the more fast of the entire school.

12. The rebels claimed to have killed more of the government's troops.

13. The boys shot the slingshots better than the girls.

14. The girls threw the ball better than the boys.

15. The man was averser to the cold than he was to the heat.

16. Trying one's patience is worser than anything.

17. I run better than swim.

18. I read X, and I read Y, but I like X best.

19. The ankle was more swole than the arm was.

20. He will have to kick it faster at the end than he did the beginning.

21. Knowing the truth now is better than finding out.

22. Going up the front is much better than the back.

23. He reacted in a civiler manner than she did.

24. He will eat as fast as he could.

25. I went there as quickly as her.

Answers to Exercise 7.23:
Faulty and Incomplete Comparisons
Directions: Correct the sentences if there's a problem, or write *C* if correct.

1. I hit the balls faster than John **did.**
2. The train is slower than the car **is.**
3. The trip to London is longer than **the trip to** New York. We do not want to compare the trip to the city of New York.
4. I would have bought the green one, because it is **shorter** than the red one is.
5. They were all running fast, but Tom was the **fastest.**
6. Swimming in the lake is better than **swimming in** the marina. The comparison is to swimming in the marina and not to the marina itself.

7. Running a long time is more detrimental to the shins than lifting weights **is.** Without any changes, the sentence indicates that running is detrimental to lifting weights.

8. I saw and liked the simpler one more than the other type. (Delete *the*)

9. The outside was cold, but the inside was **cold,** also. (Delete *-er*)

10. I run better than Mary **does.**

11. She is the **fastest** of the entire school.

12. The rebels claimed to have killed more of the government's troops than the rebels had lost to the government.

13. The boys shot the slingshots better than the girls **did.** The boys were not shooting the girls!

14. The girls threw the ball better than the boys **did.** The girls did not throw the boys!

15. The man was more averse to the cold than he was to the heat. (Delete *-er*)

16. Trying one's patience is **worse** than anything.

17. I run better than **I** swim.

18. I read X, and I read Y, but I like X better. Use **better** with the comparison of two things.

19. The ankle was more **swollen** than the arm was. (V3 as adj.)

20. He will have to kick it faster **at** the end than he did at the beginning. Without the word *at*, the sentence suggests that he actually kicked *the beginning*.

21. Knowing the truth now is better than finding out **later.**

22. Going up the front is much better than **going up the** back. Ensure that your comparisons are complete.

23. He reacted in a **more civil** manner than she did.

24. He will eat as fast as he **can.**

25. I went there as quickly as **she did.** Use the subject case, because, most often, the entire comparison will have a verb at the end.

Exercise 7.24: Dangling Modifiers

Directions: *Rewrite any constructions that modify the wrong word or seem illogical.*

1. Waking along the street, the bird flew over the houses.
2. Too young to be left alone, the parents took the child with them.
3. As he saw the sun rise, it made a yellow glow across the horizon.
4. When protective, the babies are shadowed by their mothers.
5. The man ran over the bump with a flashy car.
6. Besides being an escapee, the police wanted the fugitive for tax evasion, too.
7. In addition to hunger, the agency tackles many problems.
8. The man told the girl he loved her sitting on the fence.
9. We picked flowers up and down the street.
10. The candidate at the rear roared an answer in front to the accusations.
11. By working cooperatively, the game was won by the team.
12. The man was informed that he was no longer employed by the manager.
13. The dog that was damaged by the hurricane ran under the bridge.
14. The plant, as well as the parking lot, sustained due to the storm power loss.
15. The boy fell down the street.
16. Walking through the woods, the rabbits were jumping everywhere.
17. Down-and-out, the banker gave the homeless man some food.
18. Bewildered by his sudden wealth, the police investigated the robber.
19. Itching due to the poison ivy, the doctor gave the patient some ointment.
20. Laughing loudly, the clowns put on quite a show.

Answers to Exercise 7.24: Dangling Modifiers

Directions: Rewrite any constructions that modify the wrong word or seem illogical.

1. **As we were** waking along the street, the bird flew over the houses.
2. The parents took the child who was too young to be left alone with them.
3. The sun made a yellow glow across the horizon as the man saw it rise.
4. When protective, mothers shadow their babies.
5. The man ran over the bump with **his** flashy car.
6. The police wanted the fugitive for tax evasion besides his being an escapee.
7. The agency tackles many problems **in addition to hunger.**
8. The man told the girl **sitting on the fence** that he loved her.
9. We picked flowers up and down the street. (OK as is)
10. The candidate at the rear roared an answer to the accusations **in front.**
11. By working cooperatively, the team won the game. Keep your sentences active, and you can eliminate most problems like the one here.
12. The man was informed **by the manager** that he was no longer employed. This sentence is passive, so we need *by* + agent (*by the manager*) immediately after the clause it modifies. Therefore, the modifier will describe the structure next to it and not dangle.
13. The dog ran under the bridge **that was damaged by the hurricane.**
14. The plant, as well as the parking lot, sustained power loss **due to the storm.**
15. The boy **down the street** fell down. Which boy?
16. **As we were walking through the woods,** the rabbits were jumping everywhere. Make both clauses self-sufficient like these are. I call them self-sufficient, because they both have a subject and a verb that act independently of one another. Yet, if you write sentences with participial phrases at the front, do it like this:

present part. phrase–S –V.
Running a good race, the man excelled toward the end.

The participial phrase describes the element directly in front of it, the subject of the IC. The principle is true even with participles that immediately follow the unit they modify, such as ***The man, <u>beaten and tired,</u> gave in to the demands of the group***. Again, the principle is the same with exercise 17, although the modifier is an adverbial realized by a couple of prepositions comprising a phrase.

17. The banker gave the **<u>down-and-out,</u>** homeless man some food.

18. Bewildered by **<u>the robber's</u>** sudden wealth, the police investigated.

19. The doctor gave the patient, **<u>itching due to the poison ivy,</u>** some ointment.

20. **<u>As we were</u>** laughing loudly, the clowns put on quite a show.

CHAPTER EIGHT

Tips to Help You Ace Sentence Corrections

The most effective way to ace any test is to know what to expect. Therefore, recognizing the type of question you are faced with is imperative to your success. Following is a crash course on the structures that appear on sentence correction questions.

Answers and explanations follow the test.

1. Dangling Modifiers

A dangling modifier describes the wrong thing in a sentence.

Correct: After the police made a long search, the robber was caught.

Incorrect: After a long search, the robber was caught.

Note: The robber was not looking for himself.

Correct: We were annoyed by the winning team's singing all the way down the road.

Incorrect: Singing all the way down the road, we were annoyed by the team who won.

Note: We were not singing when the other team won. Be careful to put the phrase or clause that describes nearest to the thing that it is describing.

2. Parallelism

Basically, almost all of the verb structures need to be the same verb tense; this holds true even when the verb acts as a noun. However, this is not true when the events take place at different times.

Same tenses:

Correct: She walked along the road, ate some ice cream, and then rode the bike.

Note: these are all simple past tense.

Incorrect: She walked along the road, ate some ice cream, and had ridden the bike.

The second sentence is wrong, because *had ridden* is not the same verb tense.

Correct: Spiking the ball, upsetting the fans, and storming off the court are not ways to make friends.

Incorrect: To spike the ball, upsetting the fans, and storming off the court are not ways to make friends.

To spike must have the *-ing* form like *upsetting* and *storming off.*

Different times:

Correct: After we get up, we will go to the store.

Incorrect: As soon as we saw her, we started shouted.

Correct: As soon as we saw her, we started yelling.

Note: These are fine sentences, because the actions take place at different times.

Look for a relationship in a test question that indicates time. Assess from there.

3. Pronoun-Antecedent Disagreement

The antecedent is the one that comes before, so this is where a pronoun disagrees in number with a word that it renames.

Correct: Someone left his coat.

Incorrect: Somebody has misplaced their bag.

Somebody is singular, so we need to change *their* to a singular word like *his* or *her.*

Correct: They themselves know that this is the truth.

Incorrect: They themself know that this is the truth.

They must take the plural form *themselves.*

4. Pronoun Reference

These are vague pronouns, causing confusion as to whom or what one refers.

Correct: I gave the pencil to my brother, and got it back again later.

Incorrect: I gave the pencil and the lighter to my brother, and got it back again later.

Note: What did the speaker get back, the pencil or the lighter?

Correct: My sister paid my girlfriend a compliment by saying she looked nice.

Incorrect: My sister told my girlfriend that she looked nice.

Note: Who looks nice?

5. Pronouns: Subjects vs. Objects

The subject pronouns usually come before the main verb in a sentence, and the object pronouns usually come after the main verb and/or after a preposition. Prepositions are those little words that answer where, such as *in, at, around, by, near, over, under,* and *on.*

He was under the mat.
The mat was under him.
I saw whoever it was.
To whom it concerns is so overused.

Note: We need an object pronoun after *to*.
Who(ever) is the subject form; *whom(ever)* is the object.

 *NOTE:* Whom *goes at the beginning of a sentence only if (1) it comes after a preposition or (2) the sentence has an action verb; usually, it is in a question.*

1. Under the leadership of whoever it was, the men performed dastardly acts of terrorism.

2. Whom did you want to see? Whom did he hurt? Whom did the man address?

Let's turn the sentences around, and we can see why the sentences will allow *whom*.

Whom did you see? = You saw whom?

Whom did he hurt? = He hurt whom?

Whom did the man address? = The man addressed whom?

Whom is the direct object in these sentences. That is why we can use *whom* at the beginning of the sentences in the questions. So, look at the structure of the question.

Correct: It is he who came here.

Incorrect: It is him who came here.

Note: We need *he* in order to rename the subject.

If the verb is the only one, and it is a *be* verb, such as *is, am, are, was, were,* and *will be*, we need a subject pronoun on the right side of it.

Ex: S–V (*is, am, are, was, were, will be*)–Subject Pronoun (*he, she, it, who[ever]*). If the main verb is an action verb, we need an object pronoun to the right side of it.

Ex: S–Action Verb (*see, talk, walk,* etc.)–Object Pronoun (*him, her, you, it* [no change], *whom[ever]*)

6. Faulty Comparisons

These usually stem from simply not completing a sentence, having faulty word order, or choosing the wrong word for the number of things you are talking about.

Correct: I like skiing more than my wife does.

Incorrect: I like skiing more than my wife.

Note: I do not like skiing more than I like my wife, so the second sentence is wrong.

Correct: I love to sing more than my friend does (love to sing–implied).

Incorrect: I love to sing more than my friend.

Correct: Of all the people I know, John is the fastest runner.

Incorrect: Of all the people I know, John is the faster runner.

Note: John can only be the *faster* if there are two (no more).

Rule: For three or more, use the superlative form of comparison, even if only two groups are mentioned.

Correct: Out of the girls' and the boys' classes, Kim ran the fastest.

Incorrect: Out of the girls' and the boys' classes, Kim ran the faster.

Note: The second sentence is incorrect, because we know that there were more than two people running, even if only two classes were mentioned.

7. Adverbs vs. Adjectives

After verbs that indicate how a person or thing is, use an adjective.

Adjectives usually follow these verbs: *seem, taste, feel, appear, remain, look, sound,* and *act* (called copula verbs).

Remember: These are verbs that indicate the subject's state, *not* an action.

He seemed tired.

It tasted sweet.

He felt sad.

She appeared angry. = She was angry.

He remained quiet. = He was quiet.

He looked jealous. = He was jealous.

He sounded mad. = He was mad.

He acted stupid. He acted (as if he were) stupid (although he isn't).

He acted (like) a man. He was a man.

NOTE:

All of these sentences describe the subject, so the word to the right is an adjective, not an adverb. The adjective describes the subject; any adverb would describe the verb, another adverb, or an adjective.

Look at these same words used as action verbs, thereby requiring an adverbial, an adverb, or an object.

Seem—No change.

He tasted quickly; they were in a hurry.

Tells *how*.

He appeared suddenly from behind the car. *How*.

He remained at home. *Where*.

He looked furtively. *How*.

He sounded the bell. *Sounded* is an action done to the bell.

He acted slowly, so the boat left him.

How.

8. Subject-Verb Agreement

Because this is self-explanatory, we will deal with the sentences as we encounter them. Simply be aware of trick questions that insert a word or phrase between the subject and the verb, which must agree.

Correct: The boy, along with his parents, was excited about the trip.

Note: The singular verb *was* agrees with the subject *boy*, not *parents*, because *parents* is offset by a comma and is not an integral part of the structure.

The cats, accompanied by the dog, were begging for food.

The subject is plural, so the verb must be plural.

9. Subjunctive

The subjunctive deals with verbs such as *insist, order, want, demand, force*, and other verbs of persuasion. If a person imposes his will on another, the grammatical aspect is called the subjunctive. The sentence structure usually looks like the following examples.

This category is a major source of trick questions.

I insist you write the check now.

Person influences person + v1 (*write* = v1).

We ordered all remnants of the tyrant's memory destroyed.

Person caused thing destroyed (*destroyed* = v3[past perfect form])

I want you to respond as soon as possible.
Person influences person + *to* + v1 (*respond* = v1).

He forced the rebels to retreat.
Person influences person + *to* + v1.

I demand you withdraw your troops immediately.
Person influences person + v1.

Note that all of these follow a definite pattern.
Note: V1 = *eat, walk, fall*
V2 = *ate, walked, fell*
V3 = *eaten, walked* (regular verbs use *had, has,* or *have* for help if needed, but not here), *fallen*

Exercise 8.1: Sentence Corrections

1. The boy wanted to know <u>on the roof if it was hot</u>.
    a. on the roof if it was hot.
    b. if it was hot on the roof.
    c. when on the roof it was hot.
    d. if it was hot when we were on the roof.
    e. if the roof were hot.

2. The team laughed all the way home, sang until midnight, <u>and went swimming until dawn</u>.
    a. and went swimming until dawn.
    b. and went to swim until it was dawn.
    c. and swum until dawn.
    d. and swam until dawn.
    e. and was swimming until dawn.

EXERCISE 8.1

3. The man, <u>after he won the championship,</u> returned to his normal life.

    a. after he won the championship

    b. after winning the championship

    c. after having winning the championship

    d. after he had won the championship

    e. after he had been winning the championship

4. The man not only faked a heart attack, <u>but collected money on a settlement</u>.

    a. but collected money on the settlement.

    b. but also collected money on the settlement.

    c. but as well collected money on the settlement.

    d. but then collected money on a settlement.

    e. but collected money on a settlement, also.

5. Having escaped death by inches, <u>the ship carried the men home</u>.

    a. the ship carried the men home.

    b. the men were carried home by ship.

    c. the men carried home the ship.

    d. the men took the ship home.

    e. the men were carried home on ship.

6. I liked hiking as a child, sleeping under the stars, <u>and to get up early the next day</u>.

    a. and to get up early the next day.

    b. and to be getting up early the next day.

    c. and getting up early the next day.

    d. and get up the next morning early.

    e. and to be got up early the next day.

7. <u>He said that we would have to send a letter</u>, mail it before dark, and pay extra, so we did.

    a. He said that we would have to send a letter,

    b. He said that we would have to have sent a letter,

    c. He said that we would have had to send a letter,

    d. He said that we had to send a letter,

    e. He said that we had to be sending a letter,

8. <u>We didn't think we should send more than a dozen roses</u>, since we barely knew the deceased.

    a. We didn't think we should send more than a dozen roses

    b. We didn't think we should have sent more than a dozen roses

    c. We didn't think we should be sending more than a dozen roses

    d. We didn't think that we should send more than a dozen roses

    e. We weren't thinking that we should send more than a dozen roses

9. Located at the end of the street, <u>tourists always visit the mansion in the summer.</u>

    a. tourists always visit the mansion in the summer.

    b. the mansion is visited by tourists in the summer.

    c. the tourists in the summer visit the mansion.

    d. the tourists' mansion is visited.

    e. the tourist's mansion receives visitors.

10. Upset about his test scores, <u>the test was ripped up by the student</u>.

    a. the test was ripped up by the student.

    b. the test was torn by the student.

    c. the student ripped up the test.

    d. the student was ripping up the test.

    e. the student ripped at the test.

11. Poised to win, <u>the referee followed the boxers into the ring</u>.

    a. the referee followed the boxers into the ring.

    b. the referee guided the boxers into the ring.

    c. the referee was guiding the boxers into the ring.

    d. the boxers followed the referee into the ring.

    e. the boxers had followed the referee into the ring.

EXERCISE 8.1

12. I had logged about fifteen hundred hours <u>when the system was breaking down</u>.
    a. when the system was breaking down.
    b. when the system had broken down.
    c. when the system broke down.
    d. when the system begun to break down.
    e. when the system was broken down.

13. <u>Maybe he had not done it correctly</u>, but he tried.
    a. Maybe he had not done it correctly
    b. Maybe he was not doing it correctly
    c. Maybe he did not do it correctly
    d. Maybe he had not been doing it correctly
    e. Maybe he would not have done it correctly

14. <u>Had I returned sooner</u>, I would have found the perpetrator.
    a. Had I returned sooner
    b. If I would have returned sooner
    c. If had I returned sooner
    d. If I could of returned sooner
    e. If I would of

15. <u>If I was rich</u>, I would invest in the stock market, but I am not.
    a. If I was rich
    b. If I would be rich
    c. If I would have been rich
    d. If I were rich
    e. If I had been rich

16. With too much time on his hands, <u>the dog was walked by the man</u>.
    a. the dog was walked by the man.
    b. The dog was being walked by the man.
    c. The dog had been walked by the man.
    d. The man walked the dog.
    e. The man had been walking the dog.

EXERCISE 8.1

17. The man <u>who sees he who steals</u> is obliged to report it.
    a. who sees he who steals
    b. whom sees he who steals
    c. who sees him who steals
    d. who sees him that steals
    e. who sees him that stole

18. I am sick and tired <u>of him whining and complaining</u>.
    a. of him whining and complaining.
    b. of his whining and complaining.
    c. about him whining and complaining.
    d. about his whining and complaining.
    e. over him whining and complaining.

19. He demanded <u>her being returned at once</u>.
    a. her being returned at once.
    b. her be returned at once.
    c. her return at once.
    d. her be return at once.
    e. she be return at once.

20. She not only <u>lost but threw a tantrum</u>.
    a. lost but threw a tantrum.
    b. had lost but also threw a tantrum.
    c. lost but also threw a tantrum.
    d. but threw a tantrum, also.
    e. but then threw a tantrum.

21. <u>Tom, Dick, and me all</u> went to the game last week.
    a. Tom, Dick, and me all
    b. Tom, Dick, and me
    c. Tom, Dick, me
    d. Tom, Dick, and I all
    e. Tom, Dick, and I had all

EXERCISE 8.1

22. When a person gets home after a long day at work, <u>you think you might want to simply order pizza</u>.
    a. you think you might want to simply order pizza.
    b. he may think he would maybe simply order pizza.
    c. he may simply want to order pizza.
    d. he may want a person to simply order pizza.
    e. you would think he would want to order pizza.

23. <u>To think of they who died</u> for our freedom brings a tear to my eyes.
    a. To think of they who died
    b. Thinking of they who died
    c. Thinking of they whom died
    d. Thinking of them whom died
    e. Thinking of those who died

24. <u>I would have liked to say now</u>: Thanks!
    a. I would have liked to say now:
    b. I would have had liked to say now:
    c. I like to say now:
    d. I would like to say now:
    e. I would like to have said now:

25. We took a great deal of things with us, <u>including the childrens toys, camping gear, and the teams mascot</u>.
    a. including the childrens toys, camping, and the teams mascot.
    b. including the childrens' toys, camping gear, and the teams' mascot.
    c. including the children's toys, camping gear, and the teams' mascot.
    d. including the children's toys, camping gear, and the team's mascot.
    e. including the childrens toys, camping gear, and the mascot of the teams.

EXERCISE 8.1

26. <u>She gave directions to the boys and I for school</u>, and she left early for work.
    a. She gave directions and I for school,
    b. She gave directions to the boys and me for school,
    c. She gave directions to me and the boys for school,
    d. She gave directions to I and the boys for school,
    e. She gave I and the boys directions for school,

27. Completing the test early, <u>the proctor took all the papers</u>.
    a. the proctor took all the papers.
    b. the proctor had taken all the papers.
    c. the proctor had took all the papers.
    d. we took the papers to the proctor.
    e. we had taken the papers to the proctor.

28. <u>We cut the grass with the mower in the backyard from the neighbor's house</u>.
    a. We cut the grass with the mower in the back from the neighbor's house.
    b. We cut the grass with the mower from the neighbor's house in the backyard.
    c. We cut with the mower in the back from the neighbor's house.
    d. We cut in the grass the back with the mower from the neighbor's house.
    e. We cut the grass in the backyard with the mower from the neighbor's house.

29. Writing on the walls with the multicolored pens <u>are punishable by law</u>.
    a. are punishable by law.
    b. is punished by law.
    c. is punishable by law.
    d. are punished by law.
    e. are to be punished by law.

EXERCISE 8.1

30. Wherever applicable, <u>cigarette smoking carries a fine in elevators of $50</u>.
    a. cigarette smoking carries a fine in elevators of $50.
    b. a smoking cigarette in elevators carries a fine of $50.
    c. smoking a cigarette in elevators carries a fine of $50.
    d. cigarette smoking in elevators carries a fine of $50.
    e. smoking cigarette of $50 carries a fine in elevators.

31. The principal, the teachers' league, and the officials created a union, <u>which are called the CO-OP</u>, in order to help newcomers to the profession of teaching.
    a. which are called the CO-OP,
    b. which could call the CO-OP,
    c. which are calling the CO-OP,
    d. which is called the CO-OP,
    e. which is calling the CO-OP,

32. There are many sights in the Midwest which should be explored; the <u>Rocky Mountains are a prime example</u>.
    a. the Rocky Mountains are a prime example.
    b. the Rocky Mountains chain is a prime example.
    c. the Rocky Mountains is a prime example.
    d. the Rocky Mountains example are prime.
    e. the Rocky Mountains are prime examples.

33. <u>Unawares of the danger</u>, the soldier inched ever closer to certain death.
    a. Unawares of the danger,
    b. Unwary of the danger,
    c. Unweary of the danger,
    d. Unweariful of the danger,
    e. Unaware of the danger,

EXERCISE 8.1

34. The boy ran in yelling, "We almost ate the whole thing!"
    a. "We almost ate the whole thing!"
    b. "We almost had ate the whole thing!"
    c. "We ate almost the whole thing!"
    d. "We had eaten almost the whole thing!"
    e. "We have ate almost the whole thing!"

35. I understood, at least I'll admit it, only half of what she said.
    a. only half of what she said.
    b. half only of what she said.
    c. half of what she only said
    d. half of only what she said.
    e. half of what only she said.

36. Our instructions were clear: take the cash to the drop point; leave it under the bridge; be walking along the pier, and call at 12:00.
    a. be walking along the pier, and call at 12:00.
    b. walk along the pier, and be calling at 12:00.
    c. walk along the pier, and call at 12:00.
    d. be walking along the pier, and be calling at 12:00.
    e. be walking the pier, and call at 12:00.

37. The best time of your life is where you take responsibility for yourself.
    a. where you take responsibility for yourself.
    b. when you take responsibility for yourself.
    c. where one takes responsibility for himself.
    d. when one takes one's own responsibility.
    e. why you take responsibility for yourself.

38. The devout Catholic family hung <u>Jesus' picture on the wall</u>.
    a. Jesus' picture on the wall.
    b. Jesus's picture on the wall.
    c. Jesuses' picture on the wall.
    d. the picture of Jesus' on the wall.
    e. the picture of Jesus's on the wall.

39. Plainly visible from the lawn of the White House, <u>we could see the president</u>.
    a. we could see the president.
    b. the president was seen by us.
    c. the president saw us.
    d. the people saw the president.
    e. the president and the people saw each other.

40. <u>Flipping back and forth in the water, we saw the dolphin having fun</u>.
    a. Flipping back and forth in the water, we saw the dolphin having fun.
    b. As we were flipping back and forth in the water, we saw the dolphin having fun.
    c. We saw the flipping back and forth in the water, the dolphin having fun.
    d. The dolphin flipping back and forth in the water, we saw him having fun.
    e. We saw the dolphin having fun, flipping back and forth in the water.

41. Unable to attend classes, <u>the notes were given to the boy</u>.
    a. the notes were given the boy.
    b. the boy had notes given to him.
    c. the boy was given the notes.
    d. the notes were taken for the boy.
    e. the notes were giving the boy.

EXERCISE 8.1

42. <u>Because he was incapacitated by injury</u>, the player sat on the bench.
    a. Because he was incapacitated by injury,
    b. Because incapacitated by injury,
    c. Because he had incapacity by injury,
    d. Because he was being in capacitated by injury,
    e. After he had incapacitated by injury,

43. He <u>whom has squandered has lost</u> his gift of success.
    a. whom has squandered has lost
    b. who has squandered has been lost
    c. whom have squandered have lost
    d. who has squandered has lost
    e. whom has squandered will have lost

44. The class champion from last year plays the game <u>the most smarter of all</u>.
    a. the most smarter of all.
    b. the most smartest of all.
    c. the most smartly of all.
    d. the most of all smart.
    e. the smartest of most.

45. <u>To win, to succeed at all one attempts, and have never given in</u> make dreams come alive.
    a. To win, to succeed at all one attempts, and have never given in
    b. To win, to succeed at all one attempt, and to never give in
    c. To win, to succeed at all one attempts, and to never give in
    d. To win, to succeed at all one attempts, and to have never give in
    e. To win, to succeed at all one attempts, and having never given in

46. <u>Bought on credit is not wise</u>.
    a. Bought on credit is not wise.
    b. To be bought on credit is not wise.
    c. To bought on credit is not wise.
    d. To buy on credit is not wise.
    e. To have been buying on credit is not wise.

47. Walking along the creek sure beats living in the city, <u>commuting to work, and being trudging around in traffic all morning</u>.
    a. commuting to work, and being trudging around in traffic all morning.
    b. commuting to work and having been trudged around in traffic all morning.
    c. commuting to work and having been trudging around in traffic all morning.
    d. commuting to work and trudging around in traffic all morning.
    e. commuting to, working, and trudging around in traffic all morning.

48. <u>I was thrilled, relieved, sad, and overjoyed</u>—all at once.
    a. I was thrilled, relieved, sad, and overjoyed
    b. I was thrilled, relieved, sad, and joyful
    c. I was thrilling, relieved, sad, and joyful
    d. I was thrilled, relieved, saddened, and joyful
    e. I was thrilled, relieved, saddened, and overjoyed

49. I think it was Mr. X <u>whom said that</u> 1 + 1 = B.
    a. whom said that
    b. who he said that
    c. whom he said that
    d. who said that
    e. who it was that said

50. The people were <u>down-trodding, cast down to nothingness, defeated beyond hope</u>.
    a. down-trodding, cast down to nothingness, defeated beyond hope.
    b. down-trodding, casted down to nothingness, defeated beyond hope.
    c. downtrodden, cast down to nothingness, defeated beyond hope.
    d. down-trod, casted down to nothingness, defeated beyond hope.
    e. down-trod, cast down to nothingness, defeated beyond hope.

EXERCISE 8.1

51. Because you have annoyed me constantly, have asked me for the car repeatedly, and have begged me for money daily, <u>I have decided to expel you</u>.

    a. I have decided to expel you.
    b. I am expelling you.
    c. I have expelled you.
    d. You are expelled.
    e. You have been expelled.

52. The distinguished senator greeted the audience and <u>thanked their attendance</u>.

    a. thanked their attendance.
    b. them for attendance.
    c. them attendance.
    d. them for attending.
    e. their attending.

53. I hate <u>you talking with your mouth full</u>.

    a. you talking with your mouth full.
    b. your talking with your mouth full.
    c. your talking with your full mouth.
    d. you talking with your full mouth.
    e. your talk with your mouth full.

54. The man asked <u>would we move our car</u>.

    a. would we move our car.
    b. if would we move our car.
    c. if we would move our car.
    d. if could we move our car.
    e. if we could have moved our car.

55. The man asked point blank <u>what would we do</u>.

    a. what would we do.
    b. what we would do.
    c. what we could do if.
    d. what would we be doing.
    e. what would we have done.

56. I would rather <u>have been defeated</u> than to have given up.
    a. have been defeated
    b. be defeated
    c. be in defeat
    d. been defeated
    e. have been being defeated

57. <u>If I had took the pen</u>, would I still be here?
    a. If I had took the pen,
    b. Had I took the pen,
    c. If I had taken the pen,
    d. Have I taken the pen,
    e. If I had've took,

58. <u>The best-wrote poem</u> is always clear and concise.
    a. The best-wrote poem
    b. The best-written poem
    c. The best-writ poem
    d. The better-written poem
    e. The better-wrote poem

59. <u>Had he went to the military</u>, he'd be a man by now.
    a. Had he went to the military,
    b. Had he gone to the military,
    c. If he had went to the military,
    d. If he would have went to the military,
    e. If he had've went to the military,

60. <u>We reported the incident on the bridge to the captain.</u>
    a. We reported the incident on the bridge to the captain.
    b. We reported on the bridge the incident to the captain.
    c. We reported the bridge on the incident to the captain.
    d. We reported the captain to the incident on the bridge.
    e. We reported the incident to the captain to the bridge.

Answers to Exercise 8.1: Sentence Corrections

1. The boy wanted to know <u>on the roof if it was hot</u>.

   a. on the roof if it was hot.

   b. <u>if it was hot on the roof.</u>

   c. when on the roof it was hot.

   d. if it was hot when we were on the roof.

   e. if the roof were hot.

2. The team laughed all the way home, sang until midnight, <u>and went swimming until dawn.</u>

   a. and went swimming until dawn.

   b. and went to swim until it was dawn.

   c. and swum until dawn.

   d. <u>and swam until dawn.</u>

   e. and was swimming until dawn.

Parallelism: *Swam* must be simple past tense like the other two verbs in the sentence.

3. The man, <u>after he won the championship,</u> returned to his normal life.

   a. after he won the championship,

   b. after winning the championship,

   c. after having winning the championship,

   d. <u>after he had won the championship,</u>

   e. after he had been winning the championship,

We must have past perfect, because he won the championship prior to returning to normal life. On these questions, always look at the time relationship, especially between clauses.

4. The man **not only** faked a heart attack, <u>but collected money on a settlement</u>.

   a. but collected money on the settlement.

   b. <u>but also collected money on the settlement.</u>

   c. but as well collected money on the settlement.

   d. but then collected money on a settlement.

   e. but collected money on a settlement, also.

When you see *not only* on one side of X (noun or verb or adjective), you need *but also* on the other side, because these are correlative conjunctions. They control two things at once. They simply mean that X = 1 + 1. Otherwise, we could be tricked. For example, John is *not* Spanish, *but* Hispanic. That indicates he's not Spanish at all. This is a common trick construction.

5. Having escaped death by inches, <u>the ship carried the men home</u>.
   a. the ship carried the men home.
   b. the men were carried home by ship.
   c. the men carried home the ship.
   d. the men took the ship home.
   e. the men were carried home on ship.

The original question has a dangling modifier. It says that the ship escaped death by inches. Another common trick question, the dangling modifier has a phrase like this one above describing the wrong thing. Test-Taking Strategy (TTS): Make sure the two nouns in the sentence are the same noun, or at least talking about the same thing. All of the information to the left of the comma must describe the very first noun—the subject—to the right of the comma. Here, it doesn't, so we need to find the answer that will allow that to happen. D is wrong, because it suggests they physically picked it up (the ship) and carried it away. That's conversational English.

6. I liked hiking as a child, sleeping under the stars, <u>and to get up early the next day</u>.
   a. and to get up early the next day.
   b. and to be getting up early the next day.
   c. **and getting up early the next day.**
   d. and get up the next morning early.
   e. and to be got up early the next day.
Parallelism: We need the *-ing* ending, as with *hiking* and *sleeping*.

7. <u>He said that we would have to send a letter,</u> mail it before dark, and pay extra, so we did.

   a. He said that we would have to send a letter,

   b. He said that we would have to have sent a letter,

   c. He said that we would have had to send a letter,

   d. He said that we had to send a letter,

   e. He said that we had to be sending a letter,

No error. We need verb 1(written as *v1* in all the answers hereafter). A good way to check an answer like this is to read it and make sure the verbs are the same tenses. For example, *we would have to send; we would have to mail; we would have to pay.* It works for time efficiency.

 **NOTE:** *After a modal verb, the next verb immediately after the modal is always v1. The modals are* will, would, can, could, may, might, shall, should, must, had better, ought to, *and* need to.

8. <u>We didn't think we should send more than a dozen roses,</u> since we barely knew the deceased.

   a. <u>We didn't think we should send more than a dozen roses,</u>

   b. We didn't think we should have sent more than a dozen roses,

   c. We didn't think we should be sending more than a dozen roses,

   d. We didn't think that we should send more than a dozen roses,

   e. We weren't thinking that we should send more than a dozen roses,

No error. This is parallel. B is wrong, because, if you change the tenses, *barely knew* must change to past perfect to indicate you *had barely known* him before you sent his roses.

9. Located at the end of the street, <u>tourists always visit the mansion in the summer.</u>

a. tourists always visit the mansion in the summer.

b. <u>the mansion is visited by tourists in the summer.</u>

c. the tourists in the summer visit the mansion.

d. the tourists' mansion is visited.

e. the tourist's mansion receives visitors.

Refer to number 5. Tourists are not located at the end of the street. The mansion is. We don't like the passive. Passive means the subject is acted upon. TTS: If one of the answers is an active sentence that does not change the meaning of the sentence, choose it over a passive sentence. Here, there is no active choice that is suitable. Parallelism supersedes active voice. Plus, we have retained the gist of the passage with the retention of *in the summer*.

10. Upset about his test scores, <u>the test was ripped up by the student</u>.
    a. the test was ripped up by the student.
    b. the test was torn by the student.
    c. <u>the student ripped up the test.</u>
    d. the student was ripping up the test.
    e. the student ripped at the test.

11. Poised to win, <u>the referee followed the boxers into the ring</u>.
    a. the referee followed the boxers into the ring.
    b. the referee guided the boxers into the ring.
    c. the referee was guiding the boxers into the ring.
    d. <u>the boxers followed the referee into the ring</u>.
    e. the boxers had followed the referee into the ring.
The referee was not ready to win; the boxers were.

12. I had logged about fifteen hundred hours <u>when the system was breaking down</u>.
    a. when the system was breaking down.
    b. <u>when the system had broken down.</u>
    c. when the system broke down.
    d. when the system begun to break down.
    e. when the system was broken down.
Prior to the system failure, the speaker had gone fifteen hundred hours; then, the system failed. So, we need past perfect plus simple past to indicate the exact time relationship.

13. <u>Maybe he had not done it correctly,</u> but he tried.

    a. Maybe he had not done it correctly,

    b. Maybe he was not doing it correctly,

    c. <u>Maybe he did not do it correctly,</u>

    d. Maybe he had not been doing it correctly,

    e. Maybe he would not have done it correctly,

Parallelism: We need simple past tense on both sides of the comma. Past perfect is wrong with the first clause, because he did it and tried at the same time.

14. <u>Had I returned sooner,</u> I would have found the perpetrator.

    a. <u>Had I returned sooner,</u>

    b. If I would have returned sooner,

    c. If had I returned sooner,

    d. If I could of returned sooner,

    e. If I would of returned sooner,

This is a past conditional tense, which tells us that something did not happen. It is contrary to fact. We can say this two ways: First: past perfect = present perfect (like here).

The sentence order is reversed: Helping verb + Subject + Main verb.

Secondly: *If* + Helping verb (v3) + Main verb.

Ex: If I had returned sooner, . . .

I can put my two clauses in any order that I want.

I would have found the perpetrator had I returned sooner.

I would have found the perpetrator if I had returned sooner.

15. <u>If I was rich,</u> I would invest in the stock market, but I am not.

    a. If I was rich,

    b. If I would be rich,

    c. If I would have been rich,

    d. <u>If I were rich,</u>

    e. If I had been rich,

Conditional: This is a present conditional tense. Again, if the conditional is not true, it must be a past tense form. A good rule is this: In the clause that is not true, make that tense one time tense behind the tense in the other clause of the sentence. Compare the two sentences: (1) If he was there, I didn't see him. Note: He could have been there—it's possible. (2) If he were there, I didn't see him. Note: He was not there—impossible. He was at my house! The time tense in the impossible sounds ungrammatical, but it tells us of the impossibility.

16. With too much time on his hands, the dog was walked by the man.
    a. the dog was walked by the man.
    b. the dog was being walked by the man.
    c. the dog had been walked by the man.
    d. <u>the man walked the dog</u>.
    e. the man had been walking the dog.

The phrase to the left of the comma must describe the clause to the right of the comma.

17. The man <u>who sees he who steals</u> is obliged to report it.
    a. who sees he who steals
    b. whom sees he who steals
    c. who sees he whom steals
    d. <u>who sees him that steals</u>
    e. who sees him that stole

Man = subject, so we need *who* as subject; *him* is the object of the action verb *sees*, and *that* renames *him*.

18. I am sick and tired of him whining and complaining.
    a. of him whining and complaining.
    b. <u>of his whining and complaining</u>.
    c. about him whining and complaining.
    d. about his whining and complaining.
    e. over him whining and complaining.

The word *of* takes the object form, which is usually *him*. But, here, we want the entire phrase to be an object, so that's the possessive form *his* + two nouns (verb + *-ing* as a noun).

About won't work, because the idiom is *sick and tired of.*

19. He demanded <u>her being returned at once</u>.

    a. her being returned at once.

    b. her be returned at once.

    c. <u>her return at once.</u>

    d. her be return at once.

    e. she be return at once.

Same as number 18: possessive + noun = object of *demanded*.

20. She not only <u>lost but threw a tantrum.</u>

    a. lost but threw a tantrum.

    b. had lost but also threw a tantrum.

    c. <u>lost but also threw a tantrum.</u>

    d. but threw a tantrum, also.

    e. but then threw a tantrum.

21. <u>Tom, Dick, and me all</u> went to the game last week.

    a. Tom, Dick, and me all

    b. Tom, Dick, and me

    c. Tom, Dick, me

    d. <u>Tom, Dick, and I all</u>

    e. Tom, Dick, and I had all

I is the subject that goes before the verb *went*.

22. When a *person* gets home after a long day at work, <u>you think you</u>
    <u>might want to simply order pizza.</u>

    a. you think you might want to simply order pizza.

    b. he may think he would maybe simply order pizza.

    c. <u>he may simply want to order pizza.</u>

    d. he may want a person to simply order pizza.

    e. You would think he would want to order pizza.

A person is third person, so keep the third person in the second clause,
unless referring to separate events or people. Also, this is concise.

23. <u>To think of they who died</u> for our freedom brings a tear to my eyes.

    a. To think of they who died

    b. Thinking of they who died

c. Thinking of they whom died

d. Thinking of them whom died

e. <u>Thinking of those that died</u>

The word after *of* must be an object; only d and e work. The word before *died* must be a subject; only e works.

24. <u>I would have liked to say now:</u> Thanks!

a. I would have liked to say now:

b. I would have had liked to say now:

c. I like to say now:

d. I would like to say now:

e. <u>I would like to have said now:</u>

Simple present tense (*now*), polite form (*would like*).

25. We took a great deal of things with us, <u>including the childrens toys, camping gear, and the teams mascot.</u>

a. including the childrens toys, camping, and the teams mascot.

b. including the childrens' toys, camping gear, and the teams' mascot

c. including the children's toys, camping gear, and the teams' mascot.

d. <u>including the children's toys, camping gear, and the team's mascot.</u>

e. including the childrens toys, camping gear, and the mascot of the teams.

The plural of *children* is irregular, but you can follow a simple rule for all plural possessives. At the end of the plural part of the word, add an apostrophe: *children* + apostrophe + possessive *-s*. It's already plural, so add the *-s*. There is only one *team*.

26. <u>She gave directions to the boys and I for school</u>, and she left early for work.

a. She gave directions and I for school,

b. <u>She gave directions to the boys and me for school,</u>

c. She gave directions to me and the boys for school,

d. She gave directions to I and the boys for school,

e. She gave I and the boys directions for school,

27. Completing the test early, the proctor took all the papers.
    a. the proctor took all the papers.
    b. the proctor had taken all the papers.
    c. the proctor had took all the papers.
    d. <u>we took the papers to the proctor.</u>
    e. we had taken the papers to the proctor.

The proctor did not complete the test.

28. <u>We cut the grass with the mower in the backyard from the neighbor's house</u>.
    a. We cut the grass with the mower in the back from the neighbor's house.
    b. We cut the grass with the mower from the neighbor's house in the backyard.
    c. We cut with the mower in the backyard from the neighbor's house.
    d. We cut in the backyard grass with the mower from the neighbor's house.
    e. **<u>We cut the grass in the backyard with the mower from the neighbor's house.</u>**

Always situate the modifying (describing) phrase next to the word/phrase it describes.

29. Writing / on the walls with the multicolored pens / **<u>are</u>** <u>punishable by law</u>.
    a. are punishable by law.
    b. is punished by law.
    c. **<u>is punishable by law.</u>**
    d. are punished by law.
    e. are to be punished by law.

Writing is the subject, so use a singular verb. Chop up the sentences with your pen as shown if you need to in order to see the subject and the verb. This will decrease your time spent on each question.

30. Wherever applicable, <u>cigarette smoking carries a fine in elevators of $50</u>.

a. cigarette smoking carries a fine in elevators of $50.

b. a smoking cigarette in elevators carries a fine of $50.

c. smoking a cigarette in elevators carries a fine of $50.

d. <u>cigarette smoking in elevators carries a fine of $50.</u>

e. smoking cigarettes of $50 carries a fine in elevators.

See what is doing what.

31. The principal, the teachers' league, and the officials created a union, <u>which are called the CO-OP,</u> in order to help newcomers to the profession of teaching.

a. which are called the CO-OP,

b. which could call the CO-OP,

c. which are calling the CO-OP,

d. <u>which is called the CO-OP,</u>

e. which is calling the CO-OP,

The verb *is* agrees with *union* (singular).

32. There are many sights in the Midwest which should be explored; <u>the Rocky Mountains are a prime example.</u>

a. the Rocky Mountains are a prime example.

b. **<u>the Rocky Mountains chain is a prime example.</u>**

c. the Rocky Mountains is a prime example.

d. the Rocky Mountains example are prime.

e. the Rocky Mountains' are a prime example.

Chain agrees with *is* and with *example*.

33. <u>Unawares of the danger,</u> the soldier inched ever closer to certain death.

a. Unawares of the danger,

b. Unwary of the danger,

c. Unweary of the danger,

d. Unweariful of the danger,

e. <u>Unaware of the danger,</u>

This is an exercise in vocabulary.

34. The boy ran in yelling, "<u>We almost ate the whole thing!</u>"

   a. "We almost ate the whole thing!"

   b. "We almost had ate the whole thing!"

   c. <u>"We ate almost the whole thing!"</u>

   d. "We have eaten almost the whole thing!"

   e. "We have ate almost the whole thing!"

They did not almost eat it. They ate almost all of it.

35. I understood, at least I'll admit it, <u>only half of what she said.</u>

   a. **<u>only half of what she said.</u>**

   b. half only of what she said.

   c. half of what she only said.

   d. half of only what she said.

   e. half of what only she said.

No error.

36. Our instructions were clear: take the cash to the drop point; leave
   it under the bridge; <u>be walking along the pier, and call at 12:00.</u>

   a. be walking along the pier, and call at 12:00.

   b. walk along the pier, and be calling at 12:00.

   c. **<u>walk along the pier, and call at 12:00.</u>**

   d. be walking along the pier, and be calling at 12:00.

   e. be walking the pier, and call at 12:00.

All of the verbs are v1.

37. The best time of your life is <u>where you take responsibility for yourself.</u>

   a. where you take responsibility for yourself.

   b. **<u>when you take responsibility for yourself.</u>**

   c. where one takes responsibility for himself.

   d. when one takes one's own responsibility.

   e. why you take responsibility for yourself.

Time requires *when,* not *where.*

38. The devout Catholic family hung <u>Jesus' picture on the wall.</u>

    a. Jesus' picture on the wall.

    b. **Jesus's picture on the wall.**

    c. Jesuses' picture on the wall.

    d. the picture of Jesus' on the wall.

    e. the picture of Jesus's on the wall.

One person + apostrophe + *s* = possessive.

39. Plainly visible from the lawn of the White House, <u>we could see the president.</u>

    a. We could see the president.

    b. **the president was seen by us.**

    c. the president saw us.

    d. the people saw the president.

    e. the president and the people saw each other.

The president is the only one who was visible *from* the lawn.

40. <u>Flipping back and forth in the water, we saw the dolphin having fun.</u>

    a. Flipping back and forth in the water, we saw the dolphin having fun.

    b. As we were flipping back and forth in the water, we saw the dolphin having fun.

    c. We saw the flipping back and forth in the water, the dolphin having fun.

    d. The dolphin flipping back and forth in the water, we saw him having fun.

    e. **We saw the dolphin having fun, flipping back and forth in the water.**

41. Unable to attend classes, <u>the notes were given to the boy.</u>

    a. the notes were given the boy.

    b. the boy had notes given to him.

    c. **the boy was given the notes.**

    d. the notes were taken for the boy.

    e. the notes were giving the boy.

The boy was unable to attend. Remember: the phrase to the left of the comma must describe the phrase to the right of the comma–usually. The exception is if there are two subjects and two verbs. Then, they are usually self-supporting in terms of action, and they are linked together to indicate unity of time.

As we were walking, he was riding.

Before I went to Cairo, she had already returned.

As you can see, both sentences have clauses with separate subjects, but they both have unity regarding time.

42. <u>Because he was incapacitated by injury,</u> the player sat on the bench.

   a. **<u>Because he was incapacitated by injury,</u>**

   b. Because incapacitated by injury,

   c. Because he had incapacity by injury,

   d. Because he was being in capacitated by injury,

   e. After he had incapacitated by injury,

No error.

43. He <u>whom has squandered has lost</u> his gift of success.

   a. whom has squandered has lost

   b. who has squandered has been lost

   c. whom have squandered have lost

   d. <u>who has squandered has lost</u>

   e. whom has squandered will have lost

He is a subject; *whom* is an object.

44. The class champion from last year plays the game <u>the most smarter of all</u>.

   a. the most smarter of all.

   b. the most smartest of all.

   c. <u>the most smartly of all.</u>

   d. the most of all smart.

   e. the smartest of most.

Smartly is an adverb of manner that tells how he plays. Be careful when using adverbs. Action words require adverbs. *Be* verbs require adjectives, because they describe the nouns, not an action.

45. <u>To win, to succeed at all one attempts, and have never given in</u> make dreams come alive.

    a. To win, to succeed at all one attempts, and have never given in

    b. To win, to succeed at all one attempt, and to never give in

    c. **<u>To win, to succeed at all one attempts, and to never give in</u>**

    d. To win, to succeed at all one attempts, and to have never give in

    e. To win, to succeed at all one attempts, and having never given in

Parallelism.

46. <u>Bought on credit is not wise.</u>

    a. Bought on credit is not wise.

    b. To be bought on credit is not wise.

    c. To bought on credit is not wise.

    d. **To buy on credit is not wise.**

    e. To have been buying on credit is not wise.

We need the same tense in the infinitive subject as we have in the main verb, which is *is*.

47. Walking along the creek sure beats living in the city, <u>commuting to work, and being trudging around in traffic all morning</u>.

    a. commuting to work, and being trudging around in traffic all morning.

    b. commuting to work and having been trudged around in traffic all morning.

    c. commuting to work and having been trudging around in traffic all morning.

    d. **commuting to work, and trudging around in traffic all morning.**

    e. commuting to, working, and trudging around in traffic all morning.

48. <u>I was thrilled, relieved, sad, and overjoyed</u>–all at once.

a. I was thrilled, relieved, sad, and overjoyed

b. I was thrilled, relieved, sad, and joyful

c. I was thrilling, relieved, sad, and joyful

d. I was thrilled, relieved, saddened, and joyful

e. **I was thrilled, relieved, saddened, and overjoyed**

Parallelism. <u>We need v3 (a verbal) on all of these.</u>

49. I think it was Mr. X <u>whom said that</u> $1 + 1 = B$.

    a. whom said that

    b. who he said that

    c. whom he said that

    d. <u>who said that</u>

    e. who it was that said

The verb before Mr. X is a *be* verb, so it is subject case, which means we must use a subject—*who*.

Compare: This is he. This is she. All of these are subject case after a *be* verb. They rename the subject.

50. The people were <u>down-trodding, cast down to nothingness, defeated beyond hope.</u>

    a. down-trodding, cast down to nothingness, defeated beyond hope.

    b. down-trodding, casted down to nothingness, defeated beyond hope.

    c. **<u>downtrodden, cast down to nothingness, defeated beyond hope</u>.**

    d. down-trod, casted down to nothingness, defeated beyond hope.

    e. down-trod, cast down to nothingness, defeated beyond hope.

Parallelism. Again, they are all v3. V3 = perfect form, usually used for adjectives, such as *the half-eaten apple*.

51. Because you ***have annoyed*** me constantly, ***have asked*** me for the car repeatedly, and ***have begged*** me for money daily, <u>I have decided to expel you.</u>

    a. I have decided to expel you.

    b. I am expelling you.

    c. **<u>I have expelled you.</u>**

    d. you are expelled.

    e. you have been expelled.

Parallelism. All of the verbs are present perfect plus the object.

52. The distinguished senator greeted the audience and <u>thanked their attendance.</u>

    a. thanked their attendance.

    b. thanked them for attendance.

    c. thanked them attendance.

    d. **thanked them for attending.**

    e. thanked their attending.

53. I hate <u>you talking with your mouth full.</u>

    a. you talking with your mouth full.

    b. **your talking with your mouth full.**

    c. your talking with your full mouth.

    d. you talking with your full mouth.

    e. your talk with your mouth full.

The speaker hates your talking, the object, not the person, who is you.

54. The man asked <u>would we move our car.</u>

    a. would we move our car.

    b. if would we move our car.

    c. **if we would move our car.**

    d. if could we move our car.

    e. if we could have moved our car.

These kinds of sentences are called embedding, where one sleeps inside another.

They need to follow this pattern: S–V–(sometimes question word)–S–HV–V.

The test is tricky with these, especially in questions. HV = helping verb.

55. The man asked point blank <u>what would we do.</u>

    a. what would we do.

    b. **what we would do.**

    c. what we could do if.

    d. what would we be doing.

    e. what would we have done.

56. I would rather <u>have been defeated</u> than to have given up.

    a. <u>have been defeated</u>

    b. be defeated

    c. be in defeat

    d. been defeated

    e. have been being defeated

No error.

57. <u>If I had took the pen,</u> would I still be here?

    a. If I had took the pen,

    b. Had I took the pen,

    c. <u>If I had taken the pen,</u>

    d. Have I taken the pen,

    e. If I had've took,

Conditional. *Had* + V3 (Always!)

58. <u>The best-wrote poem</u> is always clear and concise.

    a. The best-wrote poem

    b. The best-writ poem

    c. <u>The best-written poem</u>

    d. The better-written poem

    e. The better-wrote poem

V3 is always the adjective, not v2. V2 looks like the adjective sometimes, but that is when we have a regular verb that does not change from v2 to v3.

    Ex: The quickly walked mile is good exercise.

59. <u>Had he went to the military,</u> he'd be a man by now.

    a. Had he went to the military,

    b. <u>Had he gone to the military,</u>

    c. If he had went to the military,

    d. If he would have went to the military,

    e. If he had've went to the military,

Had + V3.

60. <u>We reported the incident on the bridge to the captain.</u>
    a. **<u>We reported the incident on the bridge to the captain.</u>**
    b. We reported on the bridge the incident to the captain.
    c. We reported the bridge on the incident to the captain.
    d. We reported the captain to the incident on the bridge.
    e. We reported the incident to the captain to the bridge.
No error.

Glossary

(See page 291 for a list of abbreviations used in this book.)

Ablaut–Called gradation, the simple past tense of an irregular verb is formed by the changing of the internal vowels as opposed to the addition of *-ed* to the base form of a verb in regular verbs. See the Irregular Verb List in Supplement I.

Action verb–One that indicates movement or action on the part of the agent, usually the subject: *eat, hit, run.*

Active sentence/voice–A sentence wherein the subject does the action, usually to the direct object.

Adjective–Part of speech that describes a noun, word, or phrase acting as a noun.

Adjectival–A word, group of words, or clause that describes a noun or its equivalent, called such because it is not an adjective but functions as one.

Adverb–Part of speech that describes a verb, an adverb, or an adjective, or the equivalent thereof.

Adverbial–A word, phrase, or clause that functions as an adverb but is not one; generally answers the questions of where, when, why, how, and to what degree.

Agreement—The coordination of the subject and verb, pronoun and antecedent (word renamed); assumption through diction that audience is of like ideology.

Analogy—A comparison presented in the form of a story.

Appositive—A word or phrase that renames a noun, restrictive or nonrestrictive.

Article—*a, an, the.*

Audience—The reader of your paper or the person who listens to the material. Three kinds: (1) hostile, (2) wavering,(3) like ideology.

Auxiliary verb—Verb that helps the main verb in a sentence to indicate exact time; it is a *be* verb or, in the perfect tense, *has, have,* or *had.*

Be verb—The conjugation of the verb *be*; acts as (1) auxiliary verb with a main verb or (2) linking verb when it's the only verb in the sentence.

BOYFANS—Acronym to indicate the coordinating conjunctions that link two independent clauses. See *coordinating conjunctions.*

Brainstorming—A prewriting strategy used to think of ideas for a paper.

Causative verb—A verb that indicates the influence of one person over another or a person as the cause of something that is done to something else. Common verbs are *get, have, make.*

Clause—Usually, a construction that has a subject and a verb. There are two kinds. (1) IC = independent clause—stands alone, conveys complete thought with no other assistance (e.g., *I ate*). (2) DC = dependent clause (called subordinate clause)—requires the presence of an independent clause to complete the thought initiated (e.g., *When I ate, I was full*). Requires (in this text) the presence of a subordinator to make it a DC: *When* I ate . . . *When* is the subordinator. Note: There are verbless clauses, but we are concerned with survival grammar and easily recognizable constructions.

Colon—The sign : used to set off a series or a list or to present crucial information.

Comma—The sign , used to set off ICs, DCs, afterthoughts, or a list of items.

Comma splice—The linking of two independent clauses without a coordinating conjunction and a comma. ***It is wrong.*** Ex: *I ate, I went home.*

Complement—A word or phrase that renames another, usually subject or object. Ex: (1) subject: *I am angry.* (2) Indirect object: *I gave him, my friend, my book.* (3) Direct object: *They made him captain.*

Conjunction–A word that subordinates, combines and/or coordinates and/or correlates ideas, phrases, sentences, clauses, and paragraphs. There are three main kinds:

1. Subordinating conjunction–Called a subordinator; makes an independent clause dependent. Ex: *While* you were at the store, I received a call. Is usually a time word of duration or a preposition.

2. Coordinating conjunction–Links two independent clauses, preceded by a comma at the second clause. When moved to the initial position in the first clause, many become a subordinator or conjunctive adverb, thereby taking a different function and creating new punctuation– at times.

   BOYFANS = *but, because, or, yet, for, and, neither, nor, so*

   I left, but I came home.
   I ate, because I was hungry.
   I will go with her, or I will stay here with you.
   I ate two hours ago, yet I am still hungry.

   For = archaic: He ate, for he was famished.

   I love to ski, and I love hanging around the house.
   I do not drink; neither does he.
   I didn't stop at the market, nor did I want to attend to other problems.
   He had some coffee, so I joined him.

3. Correlative conjunction–Links two phrases of equal weight.
   Either/or. Either you stop or I will. Either go or stay.
   Neither/nor. Neither he nor I like the opera.
   Neither Sally nor her husband showed up last night.

Conjunctive adverb–These are conjunctions that act as transitions, showing some connection, either by comparison or contrast.
   Ex: *Therefore, consequently,* etc.

Diction–Word choice. There are two kinds. (1) Abstract–to speak in words that do not say exactly what one thinks; usually the modifier uses comparisons that are intangible, describing in a way that seems to be true or using flowery language. For example, to say a woman moves like a gentle wind is abstract. (2) Concrete—to speak in terms that are considered down-to-earth, describing perhaps why a person is nice, using examples that tell a true story. For example, to say that a woman who helped an injured animal is compassionate is concrete.

Note: The audience (hostile, wavering, like) determines the diction, and that determines the tone conveyed in the writing.

Dynamic verb—An action verb, sometimes called a lexical verb. Ex: *eat, run, walk, hit.*

Ellipsis—The sign … used to indicate the omission in writing or speech of words that are readily understood.

Embedding—The presence of a dependent clause inside a larger independent clause, usually with relative clauses or through an ellipsis-shortened construction. Ex: The little dog that I hurt accidentally ate the steak.

Evidentiary statement—The sentence(s) in the introduction that follow the thesis statement. The evidentiary statement gives evidence to support your thesis.

Fragment—A sentence that is not complete. Ex: After the game. ***This is wrong!***

Free writing—Prewriting strategy used to help a writer think of topics to write about.

Genitive—The possessive form. Two methods: (1) prepositional phrase (*The tears of a child cause sadness*); (2) apostrophe + -*s* (*The child's tears cause sadness*).

Gerund—Base form of the verb + -*ing*, functions as (1) subject, (2) direct object, (3) reason (adverbial).

Gradation—Called ablaut, the simple past tense of an irregular verb is formed by the changing of the internal vowels as opposed to the addition of -*ed* to the base form of a verb in regular verbs. See the Irregular Verb List in Supplement I.

Grammar—The systematic structure of words (morphology), sentences (syntax), and the different possibilities of the constructions through the rules involved therein.

Idea book—Prewriting strategy employed to generate ideas. Writer carries it with him to write down ideas as they occur to him.

Image—Like a symbol, a recurring picture that signifies something different than what it actually is.

Incubating–Prewriting strategy where the writer takes time away from the project to think over things, letting the trees be cleared to see the forest.

Independent clause–A clause that can stand alone (e.g., *I finished class at 9:00*).

Infinitive–*To* + base form of a verb; functions as (1) subject, (2) direct object, (3) reason (adverbial).

Intransitive verb–A verb that does not require a direct object.

Irregular verb–A verb that has a simple past tense that is not formed by adding *-ed* to the base form of the verb. The past tense is usually formed by gradation, a process whereby the internal vowels change. Ex: *sit, sat.*

Lexical verb–A verb that functions with action, an action verb, as opposed to a *be* verb.

Linking verb–One of the *be* verbs, called such when it is the only verb in a clause in conjunction with a subject complement, thereby linking the subject and its complement.

Logical fallacies–Errors in logic, commonly taken or posited as a basis for an argument. Logical fallacies are flaws in arguments that make them illogical. Avoid these, because they destroy the grade. Some writers use them, because they think the average person cannot see the error in reasoning. Further, these are common in advertising. See below.

- Circular reasoning–Involves using the same material for support of an argument as contained in the argument itself. Ex: *It takes a long time to write on a computer, because it is so time-consuming.*

- Ad hoc, ergo propter hoc–After this, therefore, because of this. Ex: *John started swimming last year with a shower cap on. He has practically gone bald in the past year. The shower cap must be the reason for his baldness.*

- Ad hominem–Toward the person. This attacks a certain point of logic by attacking the person who came up with it. It's very common in elections. Ex: *Senator X was late on paying back a loan five years ago, so we need to disregard his plan for reducing the federal deficit.*

- Hasty generalization–Commonly called stereotyping; attributes characteristics of one person to other persons in his same classification, including belief system, profession, nationality, and ethnic origin.

Ex: *Because Minister Z did that, all the ministers are like that.*

- <u>Red herring</u>– The body in a paper completely deviates from the thesis statement. (This should not be a problem when working with evidentiary statements.)
- <u>Begging the question</u>–The argument is based on a thesis statement that is assumed to be true but, in fact, may not be true; therefore, the entire argument is illogical. Ex: *Because 1 + 1 = 3, 2 + 2 = 6, . . .*
- <u>False analogy</u>–Telling a story to exemplify a point, in relation to a situation at hand, when the story told is really irrelevant. Comparing apples and oranges.
- <u>Either/or</u>–The writer poses an argument drawing a line between those who believe in the same things he does and those who do not. Those who do not are presented as being in some way inferior, because they do not buy into what he thinks.

Mapping–Prewriting strategy used to generate ideas.

Metaphor–An implied comparison of two different things, usually drawn out. Ex: *He crept silently, stealthily, ears back, then pounced on his son.* From this description, he seems like a cat.

Modifier–Adjective or a word acting as an adjective.

Modify–Describe.

Motif–A recurrent element in a written work. Can be a recurring phrase, image, methodical approach to form, diction, quotations, etc.

Narrator–The style in which a piece, usually fiction, is conveyed, by the use of the pronouns employed. Three kinds: (1) first person–uses *I* as the storyteller and has a limited point of view; (2) second person–employs *you* in the story to relate the events (uncommon); (3)third person–sometimes called the omniscient narrator, because the writer can jump into any person's mind, use any personal pronoun, and see all things in the story.

Object–(1) Direct object: Receives the action from an action verb. Ex: *I hit the car.* (The subject performs the action.) (2) Indirect object: Generally, the DO is required in the construction, and the IO is affected by the action from the action verb but is not directly in receipt of it. Ex: *I gave him the book.* He did not receive the giving, but he did receive the gift. A different position: *I gave the book to him.* (3) Object of preposition: *I like to swim under the water. Water* is the object of the preposition *under.*

Participle—A form of a verb that functions in a different manner than is normal. Past: *The **boiled** salmon smelled terrible* (acts as adj.). Present: ***Boiling** oil is a weapon* (acts as adj). Note: A gerund is a participle.

Participial phrase—The participle plus a noun (usually).

Passive voice—The opposite of active voice; the subject in a sentence is acted upon by the object of the preposition *by*. Ex: *He was hit by the ball.* No direct object is present.

Pattern of development—The technique a writer uses to develop a paper, and hence bring out his argument, such as comparison-contrast, extended definition, and cause-effect.

Persona—The false personality or character that a writer takes on in a written work. For example, a writer may act as if he is uneducated; then, in the last sentence of a paragraph, he will write in powerful and informative diction to make his opinions have more significance.

Phrase—A word or group of words, with a headword, that performs a specific grammatical and syntactic function. For example, *The old cat is my pet. The old cat* is a noun phrase, with *cat* as the headword, and its syntactic function is subject. Note: The headword does not need to be a noun to be a noun phrase, but it needs to act like a noun in the sentence.

Plot—The story within a story; in the midst of the major scenes, the specifics in the lives of the characters.

Preposition—Indicates the position of a noun or the reference to an action. These are some examples: *above, around, near, over, under, by*. We say this is a pre[*before*]position[*place*], because it precedes (comes before) a noun in a prepositional phrase. Many prepositions also function as adverbs or adverbials. Prep. phrase: *We sat **before our leader**. We sat **under the table**.*

Pronoun—A word that takes the place of a noun (e.g., *he, him*). There are subject and object pronouns. Personal pronouns are not included here. Major kinds:

• Relative—Used mainly to rename or describe a noun in a sentence: *who* (subj.–people), *whom* (obj.–people), *whose* (possessive–people or living things), *which* (things), *that* (people & things); it's possible to add *-ever* to indicate the person or thing is unknown (excluding *that*).

• Reflexive—Acts as (1) emphatic appositive or (2) direct object (or obj. of preposition). Singular: *myself, yourself, herself, itself, himself.* Plural: *yourselves, ourselves, themselves.* (1) *I myself am tired.* (2) *I hurt myself.*

- Possessive–(1) With object: *my, your, his, her, its, their, our.* (2) Without object: *mine, yours, his, hers, its, theirs, ours.*
- Demonstrative–*This, that, these, those.* (With no object, these are pronouns; with an object, these become demonstrative adjectives.)
- Interrogative–(1) With people (*who, whom* [Br.E. in initial position]), *whose.* (2) With things (*what, which*).

Pronoun-antecedent agreement–The agreement in the person of the pronoun used and the noun it renames. Ex: *He left his coat.*

Prose–In general, anything written that is not poetry.

Protagonist–The main character in a story, usually the good guy.

Relative–The headword that must agree with what it describes or refers to (e.g., a person or an inanimate object). Ex: *Which* refers to things unless it refers to a specific human (e.g., *which girl?*; *The man, who you pointed out . . .*). The relative headword is controlled by agreement.

Regional color–The use of colloquial expressions in a written work to give the writing an authenticity and the reader a feeling of being there. Ex: "He shore do have a good car!"

Relative clause–See above. The relative headword plus verb construction, in agreement with the headword and that which it modifies.

Satire–The use of humor to bite and tear down something or someone a writer wants to comment against; can be vicious or benign.

Semicolon–The symbol ; that is used to separate independent clauses without the presence of a coordinating conjunction. Ex: *I ate; I got sick.*

Simile–Expression that compares two things using the words *like* or *as.* Ex: *She is crafty like a fox. He is as mighty as a lion.*

Stative verb–A linking verb or copula (usually); no action.

Subordinate clause–The subordinator + S + V, same as dependent clause.

Subordinator–A word that makes an otherwise independent clause dependent; usually a time word of duration (e.g., *before, after, when*). Ex: *When I was a boy . . .*; *As he was coming home . . .*; *Whenever he arrives late at night . . .*; *After I was dismissed from class . . .*; *Before you come here . . .* WAWAB = *when, as, whenever, after, before.*

Superstructure–The entire sentence structure in which all phrases and dependent clauses are embedded.

Syntactic function–The role of a word in a sentence. For example, an adjective can act as a noun in the sentence and function as the subject if a noun is absent. Ex: *The old are dependable.*

Syntax–Sentence structure.

Theme–The general topic your paper deals with; the specific argument that is your thesis.

Thesis–Commonly called the introduction, the thesis is more aptly defined as the idea you want to argue in a paper.

Thesis statement–The statement in the introduction, under which all of your ideas in the paper fall and support. Your idea!

Tone–The idea, sound, and feeling you convey through your written work. It may not be indicative of your real opinion, but it is what the reader infers from your work due to the method with which it was written, specifically the diction used.

Transitional–A word, multiword phrase, sentence, or short paragraph that links ideas, examples, or paragraphs.

Transitive verb–A verb that requires a direct object.

Abbreviations

V1–Base form of a verb

V2–Simple past tense

V3–Perfect form of a verb

S–Subject

DO–Direct object

IO–Indirect object

DOc–Direct object complement

IOc–Indirect object complement

Aux.–Auxiliary verb

HV–Helping verb (same as aux.)

MV–Main verb

LV–Linking verb

PP–Prepositional phrase

SC–Subject complement

Inf.–Infinitive

G or ger.–Gerund

DC–Dependent clause

IC–Independent clause

Index

Notes

Notes

Notes

Notes

Notes

Notes

Notes

Notes

Notes

Notes

About the Author

Tim Avants is an EdD candidate, has two degrees in English, including a Master of Arts with an emphasis in Grammar and Composition, and is currently doing research to complete his EdD in Teaching English to Speakers of Other Languages. Mr. Avants currently teaches at Brookhaven College in Dallas, Texas. In addition, he has taught at Tarrant County College; Rose State College; Redlands Community College; the University of Arkansas at Little Rock; the University of Maryland–College Park, European Division; the University of Central Arkansas, Department of Rhetoric and Writing and the Office of Continuing Education; Yonsei University in Seoul, Korea; the Saudi Arabian Ministry of Defense; the Saudi Arabian Ministry of Education; the Saudi Arabian Department of Commerce; and the Saudi Arabian Monetary Agency. In addition to his vast and diverse teaching experience, Mr. Avants has authored two previous textbooks, one designed as a series text for Composition I and II at the university level; the text is entitled *Grammar and Composition*. The other text is entitled *EFL Grammar* and includes over fifty pages of exercises with complete explanations.

He also reads and writes five languages. Currently working on his EdD in TESOL, Mr. Avants understands the problems the language learner faces, so he presents the test-taking strategies for the student to overcome these obstacles. The student benefits from this experience, learning the most in the least amount of time.